THE HIGH ROAD MUSIC SERIES

The Chorister

THEORY AND SIGHT READING FOR VOCALISTS

by

LESLIE R. BELL, M.A., Mus.D.

ASSISTANT PROFESSOR OF MUSIC
ONTARIO COLLEGE OF EDUCATION
UNIVERSITY OF TORONTO

BOOK ONE

W. J. GAGE & CO., LIMITED

TORONTO

PRINTED AND BOUND IN CANADA
BY W. J. GAGE & CO., LIMITED
1947

FOREWORD

The ultimate aim of all music teaching is appreciation, the power to enjoy the beautiful and to discriminate between that which has lasting value and that which is of ephemeral interest only. While the hearing of much good music is not only desirable but necessary, experience has shown that, in the case of young people particularly, active performance is the surest path to a lasting love of music.

The human voice, with all its limitations, is the universal instrument for musical expression, and wherever people are accustomed to gather together to sing, there one usually finds a deep-rooted appreciation of music. In addition to serving primarily as a means of self-expression, an outlet for the emotions, and a wholesome activity for leisure time, singing contributes to improved speech through resonance and articulation, and to health through correct posture and deep breathing.

Ability to read music at sight is the key which unlocks the door to future participation. Without this power, singing or playing becomes such a burden that active interest, however strong at first, gradually dies. Fortunately, learning to read music is not an insuperable task. Music is simply a second language, no more difficult than others, and to most people more interesting.

In *The Chorister* Dr. Bell has presented the problems of tone and rhythm in logical sequence, using only music of proven worth, and has provided adequate material for gaining facility at each stage of development before introducing the next problem. He has also departed from the usual practice by embodying the essential theory of music in the sight singing examples, thus changing the mastery of these "facts about music" from a dull, meaningless test of memory to an interesting experience.

G. Roy Fenwick

Director of Music
Ontario Department of Education

iii

TO THE TEACHER

This text has been written at the request of numerous teachers and supervisors who feel the need for a more definite plan of theoretical study and sight reading practice in secondary school music. The old idea that the interest of adolescents can be held only by entertaining them is being abandoned with the realization that young people are sufficiently curious about music to welcome a course in rudiments and sight singing, provided that it is attractively organized and that it meets their needs.

Unfortunately, there appear to be on hand no texts dealing specifically with the problems of the adolescent chorister. Sight singing readers have been designed either for the professional vocal student or for the small child, and rudiments texts for the instrumentalist or the diploma examination candidate. A course of study which is to meet adequately the needs of high school students should, in the opinion of the author, be characterized by the following features:

1. It should integrate and teach as one subject both rudiments and sight singing, since they are actually two aspects of the same thing.

2. It should take into particular account the physiological and mental development of the adolescent, and his consequent tastes and needs.

3. It should recognize that the real aims of music education are to encourage an understanding and love of the art and to develop critical standards of taste. It should, therefore, bring the student into contact with as much good music as possible, preferably through actual performance, and should avoid the danger inherent in all sight singing texts—that of placing too much emphasis on mechanical drills, and of making them an end in themselves.

In preparing this book, an attempt has been made to recognize these principles. The material is presented in language calculated to be not so childish as to to offend the adolescent and not so academic as to confuse him. An effort has been made to win the pupil's interest and satisfy his natural curiosity by explaining the reasons for all rules laid down, as well as for the use of tonic solfa. Special attention has been given to those problems which the pupil is most likely to meet in his normal singing experience. Ornaments, for instance, are of little importance to the high school chorister, and have, therefore, been dealt with briefly. On the other hand, many topics such as the normal minor and pentatonic scales, although frequently omitted from rudiments texts, play a definite part in the music which the pupil will sing, and are explained carefully.

Very few mechanical reading exercises are offered. It is felt that the important thing is to get to the music as quickly as possible by means of the study of carefully graded songs and themes from actual musical literature. Over ten thousand musical examples were examined in the selection of the material for this book. It is hoped that the final choice will prove both interesting and helpful to the students. Instrumental themes, where singable, have been used freely, but the compiler has avoided the doubtful practice of putting words to them.

Occasionally, slight alterations have been made in certain melodies in order that they might be included in the graded scheme, but this has been done only where it was felt that the original would not suffer as a result. Difficulties of translation or unsuitability of sentiment have necessitated the editing of some texts. French and Latin words have, in many cases, been included for purposes of interest.

All melodies have been left in unison. The author believes that a reading problem is best mastered if the class as a whole attacks the same passage. Furthermore, for harmonic and other reasons, it is difficult to attempt graded sight reading through part songs. The aims of the sight singing and part singing programmes are not the same. The former activity is carried out for the purpose of developing technical facility, and should involve little or no rote assistance on the part of the teacher. The aim of part singing, however, is the cultivation of a feeling for harmony and blending; and if a reading problem in a part song stands in the way of the realization of this aim, the teacher is justified in offering the pupils a reasonable amount of assistance by singing with them.

Recognizing the limitations of the adolescent voice, the compiler has chosen melodies that are mostly within the range of an octave. For the same reason, it has often been found necessary to change the original key of a melody. The teacher will have to explain, therefore, why a theme from Beethoven's Sonata in C Major appears in the key of A, and so on. He may also have to alter, even further, the keys of certain tunes when giving pitch, in order to meet the needs of individual classes. If a pupil's range is even less than an octave, as it often is during the temporary changing period, he should be instructed to sing what notes he can, and to try to hear the others mentally until such time as he is able to produce them. Bass and treble clefs have been used in every lesson, since it is advisable that both boys and girls become familiar with both.

The material in these two volumes covers all the work in rudiments and sight singing prescribed by the Ontario Department of Education for secondary school music, and the five sections correspond to the five high school grades. Such divisions, however, need not prevent an instructor in another school system from using the book. The work can just as easily be divided into four sections, three sections, or whatever the situation demands, and there is nothing to prevent one covering a greater or lesser amount of work than that prescribed for any one grade. If, for example, the pupils have had an adequate training in elementary school music, they will be able to proceed with their reading quite quickly.

It is hoped that the course will prove sufficiently flexible at all times to meet every need. For instance, teachers who approve of a greater use of mechanical exercises may use the examples offered here as models for supplementary exercises of their own invention, and those who do not employ the tonic solfa system may prefer to omit the use of syllables.

A few suggestions are offered which may help those who use this book:

1. A little sight singing done *every* music day will bring better results than long sessions of practice carried out only upon occasions.

2. It is advisable to make use of all the melodies of each chapter. Pupils should read as much music as possible. It is felt that the course offered here possesses an advantage over most others in providing a much larger number of reading examples, and in thus allowing the pupils to progress at a more leisurely pace.

3. Many teachers assist the class by rote far too soon. The average pupil is generally able to solve a reading problem himself if given a fair chance. It is frequently advisable to allow him time to study a printed song mentally before being asked to sing it.

4. Ear training must go hand in hand with reading in any effective sight singing course. It is difficult to include ear training exercises in a book such as this which is to be placed in the hands of pupils. Such exercises can be best offered by the teacher himself. Hand signals, intervals played or sung, dictated exercises, and modulator drills are all valuable. A teacher will find it a useful device to sing songs from this book, altering intervals or rhythmic figures and asking the class to point out the errors. A feeling for tonality is an essential part of any ear training course. The pupils will acquire self-reliance if the teacher sounds only the keynote when giving the pitch.

5. The practice of reading a song at an exaggerated slow tempo is of doubtful value. An appreciation of the spirit of a melody is a great asset to reading facility, but such appreciation is lost if tempo or expression marks are disregarded. All marking should be studied carefully and the pupil required to build up his own glossary of them in a notebook as he proceeds. If rhythmic figures prove difficult, it is better to sing the song on a monotone for the time being than to alter the tempo too much. Another aid to reading as well as to correct breathing is the cultivation of a feeling for the musical phrase and for points of cadence. It is always well to analyze a song from the standpoint of form.

6. If the real aim of music education is to be realized, sight-reading practice should be integrated with appreciation. Attention is called to the various indexes at the end of the book which should assist the teacher in presenting lessons on such subjects as nationalism, form, biography, and the like.

7. A reading programme should never stand in the way of the other singing activities. There is no harm in teaching by rote a song containing a theoretical problem which the pupil has not yet met in his sight singing. For instance, in the present course, $\frac{6}{8}$ time, because of its difficulty, is not presented until Grade XII, but it would be a pity to deprive the younger pupils of the enjoyment of singing the many fine songs written in that metre.

8. Everything should be done to add interest to the study of theory and to prevent it being considered simply a form of mathematics. If a live discussion is carried on after the reading of the text and before the working out of the exercises, the pupils will become enthusiastic about the problems of notation and reading. The opportunities for melodic composition which appear throughout the book provide an activity that is both attractive and profitable to the student.

In the preparation of this book, much valuable help and advice was received from the music educators of Ontario. The author wishes to express his particular gratitude to Mr. G. R. Fenwick, Mr. F. D. Roy, Mr. Lawton Bird, Mr. George Smale, Mr. H. D. Perrin, Mr. J. L. MacDowell and Miss Madeline Wilkinson. He is, above all, grateful to Major Brian S. McCool, whose tireless energy and unselfish cooperation have lessened the burden of the work immeasurably.

In conclusion, it may be said that since this work was written for music teachers, it is to be hoped that they will feel free to criticize it. The writer will be happy to receive any suggestions which may assist him in future revisions of the book.

ONTARIO COLLEGE OF EDUCATION
UNIVERSITY OF TORONTO

LESLIE R. BELL

CONTENTS

SECTION ONE

CHAPTER   PAGE

1. TREBLE AND BASS CLEFS. WHOLE, HALF, AND QUARTER NOTES IN $\frac{4}{4}$ TIME. MELODIES STARTING ON *Do* 1

2. MELODIES STARTING ON *Mi* AND *So* 15

3. WHOLE, HALF, AND QUARTER RESTS 21

4. THE SLUR, THE TIE, AND THE DOTTED HALF NOTE 25

5. $\frac{3}{4}$ TIME AND $\frac{2}{4}$ TIME 34

6. INCOMPLETE OPENING BARS 40

7. REVIEW OF CHAPTERS 1 - 6 48

SECTION TWO

8. HALF NOTE AND EIGHTH NOTE BEAT VALUES 53

9. THE EIGHTH NOTE AND REST WITH HALF BEAT VALUE 62

10. THE DOTTED QUARTER NOTE. THE EIGHTH REST (CONTINUED) 71

11. SHARPS, FLATS, AND NATURALS 82

12. MAJOR SCALES. MODULATION TO THE DOMINANT 88

13. MAJOR SCALES (CONTINUED). MODULATION TO THE SUBDOMINANT .. 95

14. REVIEW OF CHAPTERS 8 - 13 103

GLOSSARY OF MUSICAL TERMS 109

INDEX OF THEORY 111

INDEX OF FORMS 112

INDEX OF COMPOSERS 113

INDEX OF TITLES 115

THE CHORISTER

BOOK ONE

SECTION ONE

Chapter 1

TREBLE AND BASS CLEFS. WHOLE, HALF, AND QUARTER NOTES IN $\frac{4}{4}$ TIME. MELODIES STARTING ON *DO*

Notation

We all know that man learned to speak long before he acquired the ability to put his thoughts down in the form of writing. We also realize that he must have been able to sing and play many years before he worked out a system for keeping a permanent record of his music. In early times, people had to depend simply upon their memories for preserving their songs. This is why so many songs have been lost to us and why we know so little about the music of such people as the ancient Greeks.

The system of writing down musical sounds is called **notation.** Notation tells us three things about the music that is to be performed:

1. *Pitch, i.e.* the actual sounds we are to hear.
2. *Duration,* the time length of these sounds, from which comes the **rhythm** of music.
3. *Expression,* which involves such matters as the degree of loudness and softness of the music, the speed at which it is to be performed, and so on.

Some of the rules of music notation, like those of English spelling, may seem to us clumsy and inconsistent. (See Chapter 8.) This is because both systems have developed over a long period of time and many of their old-fashioned devices are still in use.

The Grand Stave

Down through the years, various schemes were tried for the purpose of indicating pitch. One of these was the use of the *neumes,* a sort of shorthand system of little signs placed above the written words of a melody, as in the illustration on the right.

1

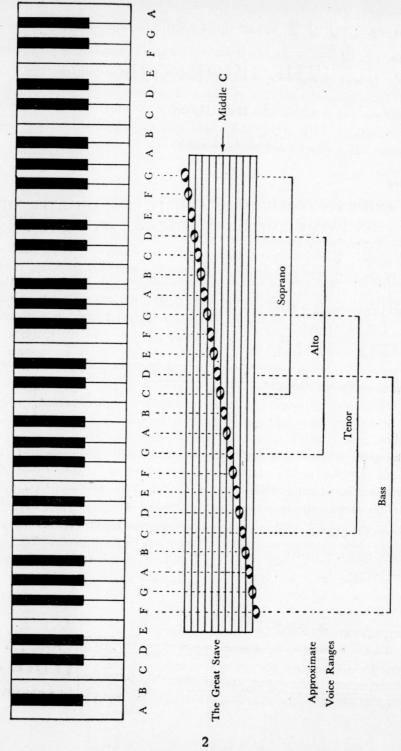

Eventually there was developed the idea of representing sounds by signs known as *notes, e.g.* ♩ ♪ ♩ ♪, placed upon a series of lines and spaces called a *staff* or *stave, e.g.* . In former times, the number of lines used varied greatly. It was thought by some that eleven lines would provide a stave big enough for the vocal ranges of all the average human voices. This was called the *grand stave* or *great stave*. The diagram on the opposite page shows the grand stave, the names of the notes, and where they may be found on the white keys of the piano. This chart must be memorized.

The Octave

It will be noted that in naming notes, only seven letters of the alphabet, A to G, are used, after which we begin again with A. The reason for this will be seen if you sound on the piano any two notes of the same name (two A's, two B's, etc.). You discover that one A, for instance, simply duplicates the sound of another A at a higher or lower pitch; whereas if an A and B are played together, you are immediately aware of two different sounds. The eighth note upward or downward from any starting point is called the *octave* of the original note. The abbreviation for octave is 8ve. Observe that when a note is on a line, the octave is on a space, and vice-versa.

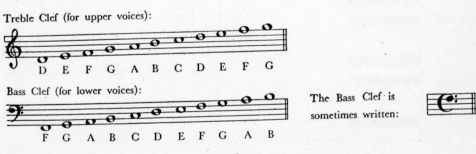

The Clefs

The great stave is actually not practical for sight reading, since it contains too many lines for the eye to follow without confusion. Moreover, no individual singer has a vocal range that requires eleven lines. Consequently the practice has arisen of having the female or unchanged boy voices use only the upper five lines of the great stave, and the male voices the lower five, thus: [staff]. In order to show which part of the grand stave the five lines have come from, *clefs* are used.

Treble Clef (for upper voices):

D E F G A B C D E F G

Bass Clef (for lower voices):

F G A B C D E F G A B

The Bass Clef is sometimes written: [clef symbol]

3

It will be seen that the treble or G clef always curls around the line G, and that the bass or F clef always curls around the line F. These two clef signs are actually modern forms of the old letters G and F. It should also be noted from the diagram on page 3 that the alphabetical names of the notes do not appear on the same lines and spaces in both clefs. The reason for this will be seen if you turn back to the diagram of the great stave (page 2).

Leger Lines

If singers wish to go beyond the ranges provided by their clefs, they may "borrow space" from the great stave by adding lines called *leger lines*:

Middle C

We note from the great stave that the centre line C is not a part of either the treble or the bass clef, but is the lower leger line of one clef and the upper

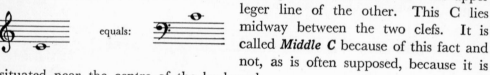

equals:

leger line of the other. This C lies midway between the two clefs. It is called **Middle C** because of this fact and not, as is often supposed, because it is situated near the centre of the keyboard.

It is possible to write a treble clef passage in the bass clef without changing the sound of it, or vice versa. If you bear in mind the position of middle C, you will not find this difficult.

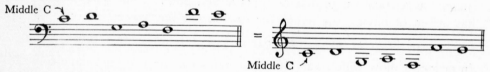

Middle C

Middle C

The Tonic Solfa System

In the last century, John Curwen, an English clergyman, developed the *tonic solfa* system for the purpose of making sight singing easier and more accurate. The tonic solfa system uses a special set of names for the notes of the staff that end on vowel sounds and are easy to sing, namely: *do, re, mi, fa, so, la, ti, do.* These are generally written in the abbreviated forms *d r m f s l t d¹*. It will be noted that small vertical lines are used to show that the solfa names have gone above or below the octave: *s₁ l₁ t₁ d r m f s l t d¹ r¹ m¹ f¹ s¹.* As in the case of the alphabetical terms, the solfa uses only seven names and then starts again at the octave: but unlike the alphabetical names, which are *fixed* on certain lines and spaces, the solfa names may *move* up or down according to where *do* is situated.

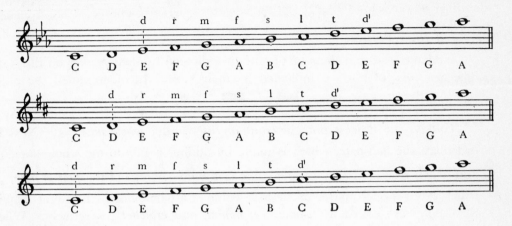

Key Signatures

The position of *do* in different musical compositions is determined by the **key signature.** The key signature always follows the clef sign and is made up of:

(*a*) One or more signs known as *sharps*: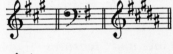

(*b*) One or more signs known as *flats*:

or

(*c*) No sharps or flats:

The full purpose of key signatures, sharps, flats, and even the tonic solfa system itself cannot fully be understood until you reach Chapters 11, 12, and 13. But for the present, the following is all you need to know:

1. If the key signature consists of sharps, the sharp nearest the music is always *ti*. By counting up one or down six from it you can find *do*.

2. If the key signature consists of flats, the flat nearest the music is always *fa*. By counting up four or down three from it you can find *do*.

3. If the key signature contains *no* sharps or flats, *do* is always on C.

Notes and their Values

We have seen that the *pitch* of notes is indicated by their *position* on the staff. The *time value* of notes is indicated by their *shape*. In olden times, the notes looked something like this:

To-day, the longest note in common use is the **whole note**: o. Next in order are the **half note,** which is made by adding a *stem* to the whole note, ♩, and which receives half the time value of a whole note; and the **quarter note,** ♩, which receives one quarter of the time value of a whole note. In Great Britain these notes are called the **semibreve, minim,** and **crotchet** respectively. When notes are below the middle line of a clef, their stems are placed on the right side and point upwards; when notes are above the middle line, their stems are placed on the left side and point downwards. The stems of notes on the centre line may point either way; it is chiefly a question of neatness and convenience.

Bar Lines and Measures

Rhythm, as we commonly use the term to-day, depends upon a succession of beats recurring in regular groups of 2, 3, 4, etc. We can feel these groups of beats in a song, in a dance, or even in the sound of a mechanical engine. To indicate this, music is divided by means of vertical lines called **bar lines** or **bars** into sections called **measures,** each

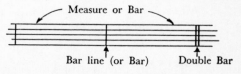

containing the same number of beats. The word *bar* is also sometimes used to mean a measure. A **double bar** is often used to indicate the end of a composition or an important division in it.

Time Signatures

Whole, half, and quarter notes each receive a definite number of beats. We are told what this number is to be by the **time signature,** which always follows the key signature at the beginning of a piece of music.

The upper figure of the time signature tells the number of beats each bar is to contain, and the lower figure tells the note value of each beat. Hence, in the above example there are 4 beats in a bar, each one of which is equivalent to a quarter note, since the lower 4 stands for "quarter note." Under these conditions the beat values of whole, half, and quarter notes will be:

This is the most usual beat value of these notes, but, as will be seen in Chapter 8, they do not always receive this value.

It will be observed by referring to the songs in this book, that the key signature reappears at the beginning of every line of a composition but that the time signature appears only in the first line.

Accent

Within each measure there is a definite system of *accents*. A careful attention to these accents will help you to acquire rhythmic accuracy, especially in the earlier stages of sight reading. In $\frac{4}{4}$ time, a strong accent is given to notes appearing on the first beat of the measure, and a lighter one to those appearing on the third beat. The other beats are without accent.

Phrase and Cadence

In addition to the rhythm of the *beat*, we also speak of the rhythm of the *phrase*. Musical compositions fall into definite sections, the beginning and ends of which you can learn to feel if you are attentive. The ability to recognize these *points of cadence,* as they are called, is essential for proper breathing and expression.

In the earlier exercises of this book, the division of phrases is indicated by *phrase marks*, as in the following example:

Good King Wen - ces - las looked out, On the feast of Ste - phen,

Musical Terms and Signs

The manner in which a piece of music is to be performed—*i.e.* its speed, its spirit, etc.—is indicated by certain terms and signs placed at the beginning of

7

a composition or at varying intervals throughout it. These terms appear repeatedly in the melodies that follow. It is important that you memorize each one as it appears. A complete list or glossary of musical terms will be found on page 109.

In writing music it is important to strive at all times for habits of accuracy and neatness. Carelessly written music is difficult to read.

WRITTEN EXERCISES

1. Write examples of a treble clef, a quarter note, a sharp, a whole note, a flat, a bass clef, and a semibreve.
2. Draw a diagram of the piano keyboard, and on it mark the position of D, B, F, A, and E.
3. Mark the lines or spaces on which *do* is situated in each of the following cases:

4. Copy out the following, and give the alphabetical and tonic solfa names of each of the notes:

5. Re-write each of the following in different clefs without changing the actual sound of the music.

6. Explain what is meant by the following time signature. Add to each bar a sufficient number of notes to make it complete.

7. Mark the accents in the following passage. Re-write it an 8ve higher and an 8ve lower, using the *same* clef.

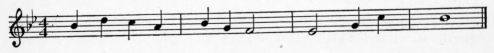

PRELIMINARY VOCAL EXERCISES

1. Sing the following to the sound of the solfa syllables:

(a)

(b)

2. Sing the following monotone exercises, paying particular attention to **beat** and accent.

(a)

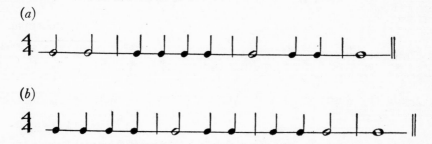

(b)

3. The following is an excerpt from a tune which you probably know. It is based upon the theory outlined in this chapter, and will help to prepare you for reading the melodies that follow.

In the moon's pale sha - dow, Lit - tle friend, Pier - rot,

Soft thy can - dle glist - ens on the fall - ing snow.

The following melodies are based on the points of theory covered in this chapter. Fix the sound of *do* firmly in your mind before you begin to sing, and observe the accent of the beat carefully.

9

Evening Song

Welsh Melody dating back to time of ancient Druids

Through the gold sinks the sun; o'er the fields sha-dows run.

Dis-tant bells e-cho long, "Day is done. Day is done."

Lord, Thy Word Abideth

Baker

Bohemian Hymn

Lord, Thy word a - bi - deth, and our foot-steps gui - deth.

Who its truth be - liev - eth light and joy re - ceiv - eth

Theme from the "Academic Festival Overture"

NOTE.—The sign > over a note indicates that it is to receive a special accent or emphasis.

Brahms

Hunting Song

From a manuscript of
Henry VIII's time

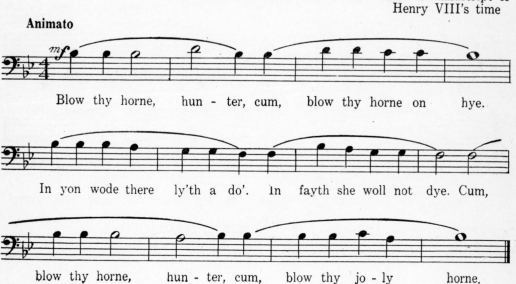

Animato

Blow thy horne,   hun - ter, cum,   blow thy horne on   hye.

In yon wode there   ly'th a do'.   In   fayth she woll not   dye. Cum,

blow thy horne,   hun - ter, cum,   blow thy jo - ly   horne.

Chorale

J. Newton

From "Thommen's Chorale Book" (1745)

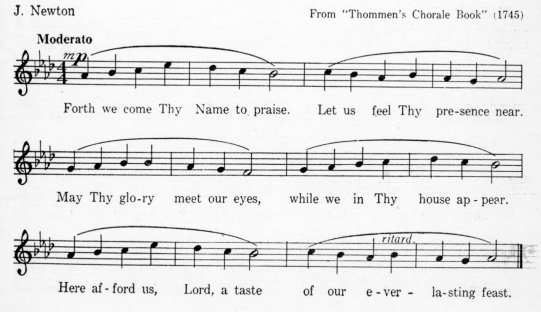

Moderato

Forth we come Thy   Name to praise.   Let us   feel Thy   pre-sence near.

May Thy glo-ry   meet our eyes,   while we   in Thy   house ap - pear.

Here af - ford us,   Lord, a taste   of   our   e - ver -   la-sting feast.

Submission

NOTE.---The sign ⟍ indicates a diminuendo or softening of tone. ⟋ indicates the reverse.

Procter

Peace

Andante

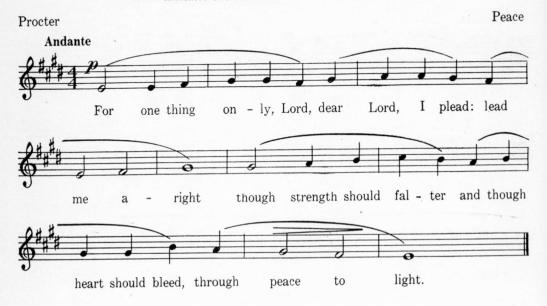

For one thing on - ly, Lord, dear Lord, I plead: lead

me a - right though strength should fal - ter and though

heart should bleed, through peace to light.

The Broken Tryst

Welsh Melody

Andantino

Sad by a foun - tain sat a la - dy fair;

watch'd for her lo - ver who would meet her there.

Blue were her eyes, and gol - den was her hair.

Wept for her lo - ver, gone she knew not where.

12

Tally Ho!

French Folk Tune

Marcato

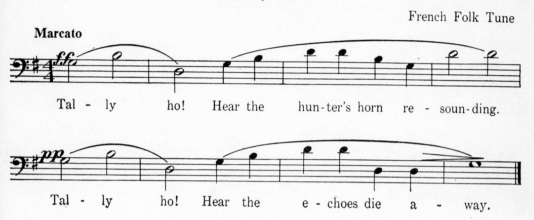

Tal - ly ho! Hear the hun-ter's horn re - soun-ding.

Tal - ly ho! Hear the e - choes die a - way.

The Eagle

Anonymous (1609)

Andante

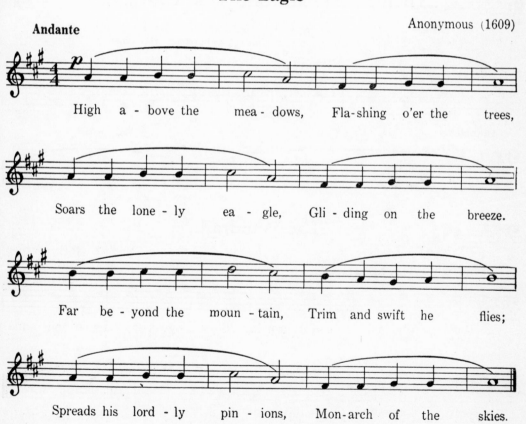

High a - bove the mea - dows, Fla-shing o'er the trees,

Soars the lone - ly ea - gle, Gli - ding on the breeze.

Far be - yond the moun - tain, Trim and swift he flies;

Spreads his lord - ly pin - ions, Mon-arch of the skies.

13

Now the Day Is Over

S. Baring-Gould

Anonymous

Now the day is o - ver, Night is draw-ing nigh;

Sha-dows of the eve - ning Steal a - cross the sky.

Theme adapted from "Don Giovanni"

NOTE.—A double bar preceded by dots indicates that the singer :‖
is to return to the beginning and repeat the passage.

Mozart

The Windmill

English (16th century)

High the wind-mill, e-ver turn-ing, Slow-ly creak-ing round and round.

Fields be-low and shin-ing ri - ver Soft-ly e - cho back the sound.

Chapter 2

MELODIES STARTING ON *MI* AND *SO*

Common Time

$\frac{4}{4}$ time is often called **common time,** and frequently the symbol C is used instead of $\frac{4}{4}$. Many people think this is the letter C standing for "common." Actually it is a form of the old semicircle that used to be used as a time signature.

The melodies that follow (pages 15-17) start on *mi*. Before singing them, be sure that the sound of *do* is firmly fixed in your mind. Another name for *do* is the **keynote**.

The following is a familiar tune which starts on *mi*:

Now the day is ov - er, Night is draw - ing nigh,

Sha - dows of the eve - ning steal a - cross the sky.

Winter Night

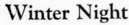

Filitz

Cantabile

Win - ter sky at mid - night, si - lent and se - rene,

Vis - tas dim of star - light o'er a moon - lit scene.

15

Theme from the Sonata in C Major*

Allegro

Beethoven

*For explanation of this and other key changes see page VI.

Cossack Dance

Allegro vivace

Reverence

Tersteegen

Joachim Neander
(1640-1680)

Andante

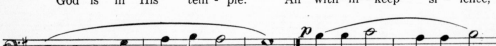

God re-veals His   pre - sence.   Let us now a - dore Him,
God is in His   tem - ple.   All with- in keep   si - lence,

And with awe ap - pear be-fore   Him.   Him a-lone,   God we own,
Pro-strate lie with dee-pest re - v'rence.

Him our God and   Sa - viour: Praise His name for   e - ver.

16

Theme (adapted)

Allegro con brio

Pleyel
(1758-1831)

Evening

Heber

Henry Monk

Con espressione

God, that ma-dest earth and hea - ven, Dark - ness and light,
Who the day for toil hast gi - ven, For rest the night,

May Thine an-gel guards de-fend us, Slum-ber sweet Thy mer-cy send us,

Ho - ly dreams and hopes at - tend us, This live-long night.

The following melodies (pages 18-20) start on *so*. Once again, keep *do* firmly fixed in your mind.

Spanish Folk Song

Andantino

Thro' the ci - ty streets when ev -'ning sha - dows fall,

Sing - ing as I go, I light the lan - terns tall.

Polish Hymn

Cowdrey

Sostenuto

Praise ye the Lord. Oh! Come to - day with sing - ing.

Bless ye the Lord, all ho - nour to Him bring - ing.

Come, all ye chil - dren, His great love pro - claim - ing,

Kneel and a - dore Him. Ho - ly is His Name.

From *Fifth Book of Songs*, by Robert Foresman, used by permission of the publishers, The American Book Company, owners of the copyright.

Theme from the Nocturne in G Minor

NOTE. — A nocturne or "night piece" is a composition of a quiet character.

Chopin

Aura Lee

Old American Song

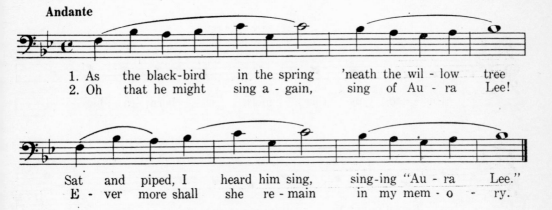

1. As   the black-bird   in the spring   'neath the wil - low   tree
2. Oh   that he might   sing a - gain,   sing of Au - ra   Lee!

Sat   and   piped, I   heard him sing,   sing-ing "Au - ra   Lee."
E - ver   more shall   she re - main   in my mem - o - ry.

Hosanna!

Palestrina

Ho - san - na   in   the   high - est!

Ho - san - na   in   the   high - est!

Carol

French

Giocoso

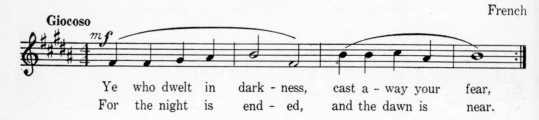

Ye who dwelt in dark - ness, cast a - way your fear,
For the night is end - ed, and the dawn is near.

Heark-en to the ti - dings, ti - dings of great joy:

Un - to us this morn is born a bles - sed

boy. Sing ye "No - el!" Sing ye "No - el!" Glo - ry,

praise, and hon - our to Je - sus Christ, the King!

WRITTEN EXERCISES

Try to compose:

1. A melody of four bars starting on *do*.
2. A melody of four bars starting on *mi*.
3. A melody of four bars starting on *so*.

Chapter 3

WHOLE, HALF, AND QUARTER RESTS

A period of silence in music is called a *rest.* There are rests corresponding in time value to the whole, half, and quarter notes.

whole note   whole rest   half note   half rest   quarter note   quarter rest

Be careful not to confuse the whole-note rest, which always hangs from the fourth line, with the half-note rest, which always lies on the third line.

Rests should not be so placed in a bar that they cover up the beats on which the accents fall, otherwise the music becomes difficult to read.

The second accent is hidden.   The second accent can be seen.

A rest of two bars is indicated by a vertical line and a rest of more than two bars by a horizontal line with a number above it.

Rests are just as important as notes and should be observed carefully. The common tendency of many

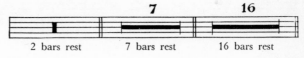

2 bars rest   7 bars rest   16 bars rest

singers to allow notes to run over into the rests always results in a slovenly performance.

WRITTEN EXERCISES

1. Add correct rests to the following so that each bar will be complete:

2. Re-write the following, correcting the errors:

Sing on a monotone:

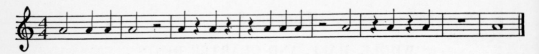

On the Bridge of Avignon

French Folk Song

Con spirito

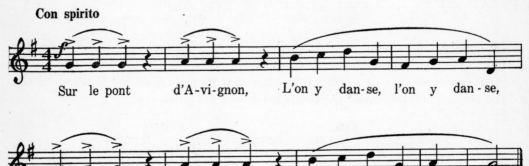

Sur le pont d'A-vi-gnon, L'on y dan-se, l'on y dan-se,

Sur le pont d'A-vi-gnon, L'on y dan-se tout en rond.

Lithuanian Folk Dance

Ben marcato

Country Dance

NOTE. In this song the last four bars are repeated; *i.e.*, the sign :‖ indicates that the singer should return to ‖: , and not to the beginning (compare page 14).

Con energia

Bavarian Folk Tune

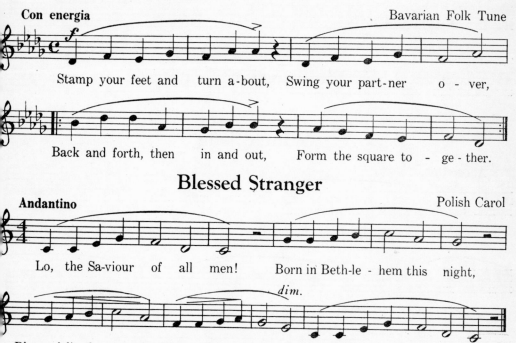

Stamp your feet and turn a-bout, Swing your part-ner o - ver,

Back and forth, then in and out, Form the square to - ge - ther.

Blessed Stranger

Andantino

Polish Carol

Lo, the Sa-viour of all men! Born in Beth-le - hem this night,

Bless-ed lit-tle stran-ger, Crad-led in a man-ger 'Neath the hea-vens' star-ry light.

Wake, Awake—Chorale (adapted)

NOTE.—The sign ⌢ indicates a pause. The note is to be held at the performer's or conductor's pleasure.

Nicolai

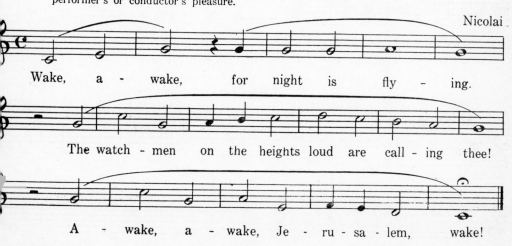

Wake, a - wake, for night is fly - ing.

The watch - men on the heights loud are call - ing thee!

A - wake, a - wake, Je - ru - sa - lem, wake!

23

Theme from the Overture to "Romeo and Juliet"

Tschaikowsky

Lento

Winter Song

Magyar Folk Tune

Allegretto

Win - ter wind a - blow-ing,   a - blow-ing,   a -

blow-ing,   Win - ter wind a - blow-ing,   shin-ing fields be -

low,   Down-y   snow-flakes   dan-cing as   they   go,

Sleigh-bells'   ting - a - ling,   glid - ing o'er   the   snow.

Theme

Pleyel

Allegro moderato

Chapter 4

THE SLUR, THE TIE, AND THE DOTTED HALF NOTE

The Slur

You are already familiar with the phrase sign. A sign very similar to it in appearance is the *slur*. The slur is used to indicate that more than one note is to be sung on a single word syllable. A breath is never taken between notes linked by a slur. Do not confuse the slur and the phrase mark when they appear at the same time.

The Volga

Russian Folk Song

Roll—— on-ward, migh-ty ri-ver, Roll — grand-ly on-ward,

Mile on mile thro' hill and prai-rie, Roll — brave-ly on-ward.

The Watchers

Polish Folk Song

Sing soft — mu - sic as the sha-dows fall,

Sing soft — mu - sic as the night birds call. 'Till the dawn comes

creep - ing, Long vi - gil we are keep - ing Be-neath the tree tops tall.

Hallelujah!

Bateman

Spanish

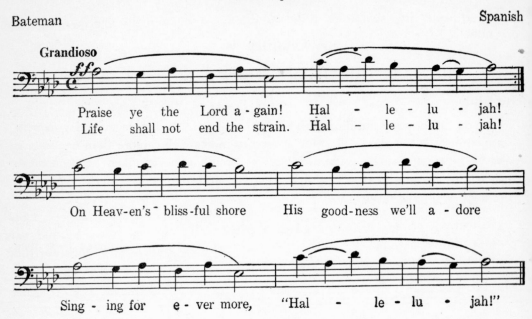

Grandioso

Praise ye the Lord a - gain! Hal - le - lu - jah!
Life shall not end the strain. Hal - le - lu - jah!

On Heav-en's bliss-ful shore His good-ness we'll a - dore

Sing - ing for e - ver more, "Hal - le - lu - jah!"

Puer Nobis

Old Carol

'Con brio

Pu - er no - bis nas - ci - tur, Rec - tor an - ge -
Un - to us is born a son, King of choirs su -

lo - rum, In hoc mun - do pas - ci - tur Do -
per - nal. See on earth His life be - gun, Of

mi - nus Do - mi - no - - - - - rum.
lords the Lord e - ter - - - - - nal.

26

The Tie

If a slur links two notes of the same pitch, it will actually join them into one note.

This sounds the same as:

Glo - ry be — to — Thy — Name!

Glo - ry be to — Thy Name!

The slur sign thus used is called a *tie*.   The tie serves three important uses:

1. In some songs, different verses use a different number of syllables.   Consequently, we might, for instance, require a half note in one verse and two quarter notes at the same spot in the next verse.   The tie helps to show the time value for the different verses.

The Lonely Swan

Russian Folk Song

Allegro
mf

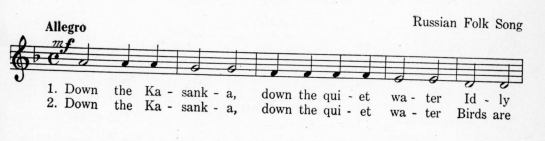

1. Down   the Ka - sank - a,   down the qui - et   wa - ter   Id - ly
2. Down   the Ka - sank - a,   down the qui - et   wa - ter   Birds are

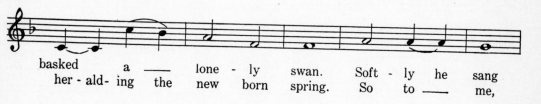

basked   a ——   lone - ly   swan.   Soft - ly he   sang
her - ald- ing   the   new   born   spring.   So   to ——   me,

to   the   qui - et   wa - ter.   Sad was the   note   of his   dy - ing   song.
by   the   qui- et   wa - ter,   Life   is —   sweet, and of   joy   I   sing.

27

When the Wind is in the East

Old English Folk Tune

Animato

1. When the wind is in the east, 'Tis nei - ther good for
2. When the sun is . shin - ing, Then in the wood re-

man nor beast, 'Tis nei - ther good for man nor beast.
clin - ing, I take my ease, and all is peace.

Christmas Song

Hauptmann

Con anima

mf

1. Sing — ye, sing ye, all the world re - joi - ces. —
2. Heark-en ye souls to the an - gel voi - ces tell - ing how

Sing ye, sing — ye, — on this bless - ed morn.
On this hap - py day a Sa - viour is born.

The Wanderer

Hungarian Folk Song

Con tenerezza

1. Far from thee — to the shores a-cross the sea Long and far I wan-dered
2. Soon a - gain shall I come — to — thee. In each scene — thy —

for-tune beck-oned me. Snow 'mid twi-light fall-ing, thy green
face — do I see. Snow 'mid twi-light fall-ing, thy green

hills re-call-ing, Sad eyes — fill with tears as, dream-ing, thee I see.
hills re-call-ing, Glad eyes will light with smiles when once a - gain with thee

2. A tie makes it possible to extend the length of a note over the edge of a bar line. This frequently robs the first note in a bar of its natural strong accent and produces an effect called *syncopation*.

Theme adapted from the Quartet in A

Andante cantabile

Beethoven

rall.

Lord, We Are Few

William Cowper

Lowell Mason
From a Gregorian Chant

Larghetto

Lord, we are few but Thou art near, Nor short Thine

arm nor deaf Thine ear. O, rend the Heav'ns, come

rit.

quick - ly down, And make a thou - sand hearts Thine own.

Theme adapted from the Arioso

Grazioso

J. S. Bach

3. The tie enables us to create notes of various beat values which we might not otherwise possess.

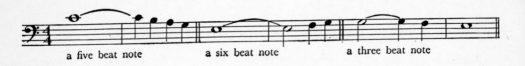

a five beat note   a six beat note   a three beat note

The Dotted Half Note

There is, however, another way of indicating that a note has three beats in $\frac{4}{4}$ time. A *dot* placed after any note increases its time value by one-half. Hence a dotted half note in $\frac{4}{4}$ time receives three beats.

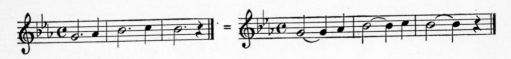

A half rest may be dotted in the same way, but it is not much used in $\frac{4}{4}$ time, since it covers up the second accent. (Compare the example on page 21.)

poor   good

WRITTEN EXERCISES

1. Re-write the following melody so that it will fit the words of both verses:

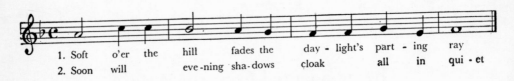

1. Soft   o'er   the   hill   fades the   day - light's   part - ing   ray
2. Soon   will   eve -ning sha- dows   cloak   all   in   qui - et

2. Re-write the following, substituting dots for ties:

3. In $\frac{4}{4}$ time, write examples of a five beat note, a seven beat note, and an eight beat note.

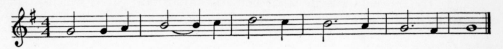

A Familiar Tune

Lead, kind-ly Light, a - mid th'en - circ - ling gloom, lead Thou me on.

Roses I Bring

Hauptmann

Con amore

Ro - ses I bring to you my fair - est

one. ___ My love to pledge ___ till life is done.

The Captive

Russian Folk Song

Dolente

Comes ___ the gold-en glow of mor - ning light, Ne'er ___ its

beau - ty shall I see. ___ Here in my dun-geon cell a

lone I sit, ___ And e - ver turns my heart to thee. ___

31

The Forty-Second Psalm

French Chant

Moderato

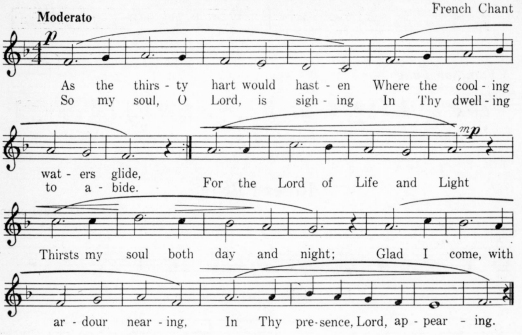

As the thirs-ty hart would hast-en Where the cool-ing
So my soul, O Lord, is sigh-ing In Thy dwell-ing

wat-ers glide,
to a-bide. For the Lord of Life and Light

Thirsts my soul both day and night; Glad I come, with

ar-dour near-ing, In Thy pre-sence, Lord, ap-pear-ing.

From *Fifth Book of Songs*, by Robert Foresman, used by permission of the publishers, The American Book Company, owners of the copyright.

Night

Czechoslovakian Folk Song

Andante

Dark a-gainst the sky the gloo-my fir trees si-lent stand.

Dark a-gainst the sky the dis-tant moun-tains rise.

In the west the sun-set glo-ry tells the end of day-light's sto-ry.

morendo

Soon the stars will shine a-bove the fields on high.

Theme from "La Traviata"

NOTE.—This melody has a fairly wide range. If you cannot sing the highest notes, try to hear them in your mind.

Verdi

Moderato

The Dancers

Serbian Folk Song

Allegro energico

See the dan - cers gai - ly sway - ing Whirl - ing to and
fro. Hear the fly - ing fid - dles play - ing,
mer - ry tunes we know. Hear the fly - ing
fid - dles play - ing, mer - ry tunes we know.

Chapter 5

¾ TIME AND ²⁄₄ TIME

¾ *Time*

Review pages 6 and 7. The time signature $\frac{3}{4}$ indicates that there are 3 beats to a bar, each equivalent to a quarter note. The strong accent falls on the first beat of the bar, and the weak accent falls on the third beat.

WRITTEN EXERCISE

Change the position of the bar lines in the following so that it will be in $\frac{3}{4}$ time. Mark the new accents.

A Familiar Tune

Gold - en slumb - ers, kiss your eyes,

Un Canadien errant

A. Gérin-Lajoe   French Canadian Folk Song

Un Ca - na - dien er - rant Ban - ni de ses fo - yers,

Par-cou - rait en pleu - rant, Des pa - ys é - tran - gers,

Par - cou - rait en pleu - rant, Des pa - ys é - tran - gers.

Praise to the Lord

Translation by Winkworth

Stralsund Gesängbuch (1665)

Maestoso

Praise to the Lord, the Al - migh - ty, the
O my soul, praise Him for He is thy

King of Cre - a - tion! All ye who hear, bro-thers and
health and sal - va - tion!

rall.

sis-ters, draw near. Praise Him in glad a - do - ra - tion.

Down in the Valley

Kentucky Mountain
Folk Song

Poco allegro

mf

1. Down in the val - ley, the val - ley so low,
2. Ro - ses are bloom - ing, bloom-ing so fair,

Hang your head o - ver, hear the wind blow.
Nodd - ing their heads in sweet frag - rant air.

Hear the wind blow, dear, hear the wind blow.
Day - time brings sun - shine, night - time the dew.

Hang your head o - ver, hear the wind blow.
An - gels in Heav - en know I love you.

From *Sixth Book of Songs* by Robert Foresman, used by permission of the publishers, The
American Book Company, owners of the copyright.

35

The Strife is O'er

Palestrina

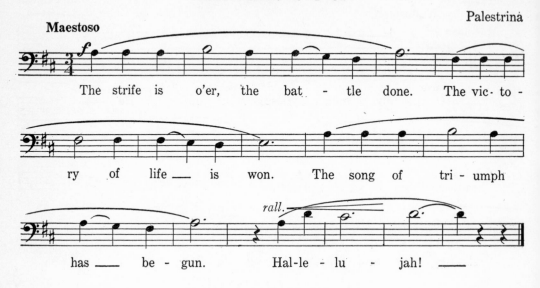

Maestoso

The strife is o'er, the bat - tle done. The vic-to-ry of life — is won. The song of tri - umph has — be - gun. Hal-le - lu - jah! —

rall.

Stand for the King

NOTE.—This same melody appears as a drinking song in *The Beggar's Opera.*

Old French Tune

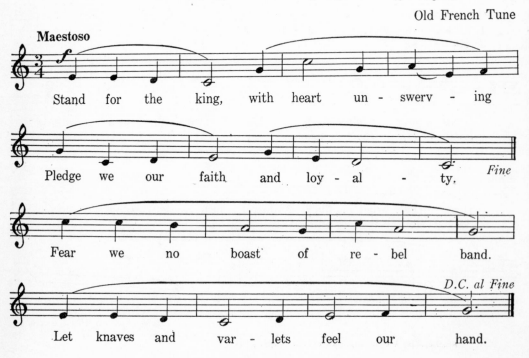

Maestoso

Stand for the king, with heart un - swerv - ing

Pledge we our faith and loy - al - ty. *Fine*

Fear we no boast of re - bel band.

D.C. al Fine

Let knaves and var - lets feel our hand.

Minuet

Allegretto

Old English

Recollections

Andante con moto

Czech Folk Song

When we re - mem - ber the friends we knew so
Hap - pi - ness ling - ered the long day through, and

long — a - go,   Ten - der thoughts,   tear   dimm'd eyes,
years — were slow;

fond   re - grets,   wist - ful   sighs,   When we re -

mem - ber   the   friends   we   knew   so   long — a - go.

$\frac{2}{4}$ Time

$\frac{2}{4}$ time should present no difficulties. There is a strong accent on the first
beat. It should be noted that a full bar's rest in $\frac{2}{4}$ or $\frac{3}{4}$ time (and in the other
forms to appear later) is written thus: ▭ , even though the bars do
not contain the equivalent of a whole note.

Song of the Emigrés

Old French

Seek we the seas un - chart - ed, Dare
Fades in the mist be - hind us All

we the might - y foam. May daunt-less hearts be
that we called our home.

ours, ___ as lands un - known we face. God

grant we may be wor - thy of His un - bound-ing grace.

Veni Sancte Spiritus

Palmer

From a 13th Century Chant

Moderato

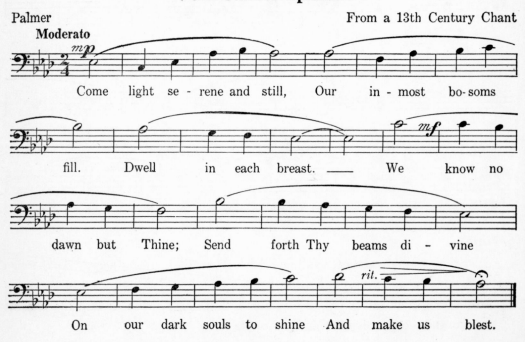

Come light se - rene and still, Our in - most bo - soms

fill. Dwell in each breast. ___ We know no

dawn but Thine; Send forth Thy beams di - vine

On our dark souls to shine And make us blest.

38

Theme from the Valse in A♭

Chopin

Moderato

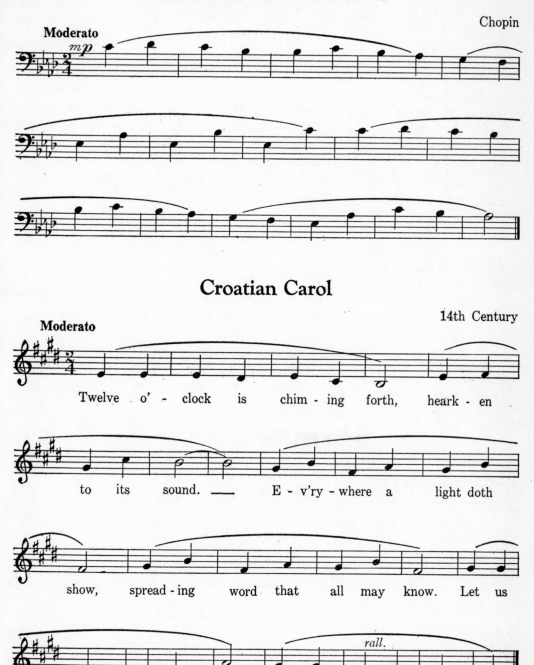

Croatian Carol

14th Century

Moderato

Twelve o' - clock is chim - ing forth, heark - en
to its sound. ____ E - v'ry - where a light doth
show, spread - ing word that all may know. Let us
all re - joice. ____ Let us all re - joice. ____

rall.

Chapter 6

INCOMPLETE OPENING BARS

A great many musical works, instead of starting on the first beat of the bar, start on the second, third, or fourth beat, thus leaving the opening bar incomplete. In such cases, the missing beats are generally found in the last bar, in order that the phrases may be balanced. You will notice as you proceed that in a great deal of music, the beginning or end of a phrase does not necessarily correspond to the beginning or end of the bar line. Notice where the phrase marks fall in the following example:

The following melodies start on the fourth beat of the bar. Count out the other three beats mentally before beginning to sing.

Chorale: The Morning Star

Nicolai-Bach

From *Motets and Chorales for Treble Choirs*, Published and Copyrighted by Hall & McCreary Company, Chicago.

40

Theme

Amabile   *p*   **Schumann**

Sherwood Forest

Allegro con brio   **Old English**

Where dai-sies grow and grass is green be - neath the stout oak's shade

With tu - nic of Lin - coln green, with long bow taut and
With Ro - bin and Fri - ar Tuck they chase the stag from

ar - row keen, There dwells a band of mer-ry men in Sher-wood's glade.
dawn to dusk, A com-pan - y of mer-ry men in Sher-wood's glade.

Theme from the Piano Trio in B

Brahms

Allegro con brio

Sea Shanty

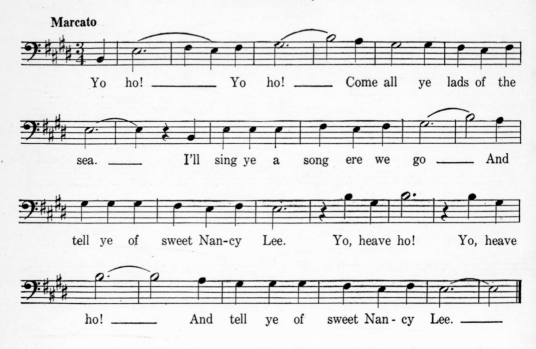

Marcato

Yo ho! ———— Yo ho! ———— Come all ye lads of the

sea. ——— I'll sing ye a song ere we go ——— And

tell ye of sweet Nan-cy Lee. Yo, heave ho! Yo, heave

ho! ——— And tell ye of sweet Nan-cy Lee. ———

All Ye That Are Good Fellows

Old English Ballad

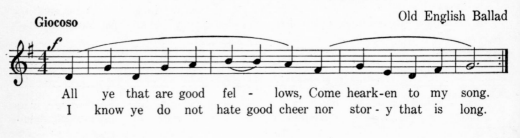

Giocoso

All ye that are good fel - lows, Come heark-en to my song.
I know ye do not hate good cheer nor stor - y that is long.

And if there be some here who've heard it all be - fore, I

pray that they will bear with me and call a - gain for more.

Theme from the "Pathétique" Symphony

Andante lamentoso   Tschaikowsky

Theme from the "Requiem"

Con moto   Brahms

The following melodies start on the third beat of the bar. Count out the
two missing beats before singing.

Bound to Alabama

Con anima   Sea Shanty

Oh! I'm   boun' ter A - la - ba - ma Ter   roll the cot - ton

down, — I'm boun' ter A - la - ba - ma Ter   roll the cot-ton down.

From *Songs of Sea Labour* by E. T. Bullen and W. F. Arnold, used by permission of the
Copyright owners, Swan & Co. (Music Publishers) Ltd.

Melody

Beethoven

Alleluia

From "The Cherubim Song"

Tschaikowsky

Al - le - lu - ia, Al - le - lu - ia, Al - le -

lu - ia, Al - le - lu - ia, Al - le - lu - ia, Al - le -

lu - ia, Al - le - lu - ia, Al - le - lu - ia, Al - le -

lu - ia, Al - le - lu - ia, Al - le - lu - ia!

Theme from "The Faery Queen"

Andante

Purcell

Yodelling Song

Allegro

Swiss Folk Tune

Where the snow - y moun - tain tree pokes its head up to the

sky, There Ka - trin - ka waits for me, I shall see her bye and

bye. O - yoo - lay - ee - ay - ee - ay - ee - ay - ee - ay - ee -

O! O - yoo - lay - ee - ay - ee - ay - ee - ay - ee - O! ___

The following melodies start on the second beat of the bar.

A *Familiar Tune*

Can you name it?

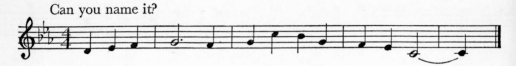

Serenade

Russian Folk Song

Con tenerezza

Gui - tar and I are come to se - re -
nade thee Be - fore thy win - dow,
fair one, in the night, A song of
love and long - ing have I made thee;
In ten - der tones 'twill tell thy lo - ver's plight. ____

From *Fifty Russian Folk Songs* by E. L. Swerkoff, English version by D. Millar Craig, used by permission of Novello & Company, Ltd., London.

The Linden in the Dale

Andante

Spicker

mp

Ah, lin-den stand-ing in the dale, What art thou do-ing here? Wouldst try to help me sor-row, sor - - row, That I have lost my lo-ver dear?

From *Songs of Germany* by Max Spicker, English translation by H. G. Chapman. Copyright, 1904, by G. Schirmer, Inc. Copyright renewal assigned, 1932, to G. Schirmer, Inc.

Chorale

J. S. Bach

Maestoso

Whose hope and trust doth lie in God Hath built u-pon a rock sure, Hath built u-pon a rock sure. ——

WRITTEN EXERCISE

Compose a melody of at least four bars starting on an incomplete bar.

Chapter 7

REVIEW OF CHAPTERS 1-6

WRITTEN EXERCISES

1. In the bass clef write the notes B, F, C, A, and E. Place at least two of them on leger lines.
2. Select either of the melodies on page 29, which are written in the treble clef. Rewrite it an octave lower in the bass clef.
3. Write out at least 4 bars in $\frac{4}{4}$ time, including in them examples of the whole, half, and quarter note, and the whole, half, and quarter rest.
4. Write:
   (a) Two musical terms which indicate that a song is to be sung quickly.
   (b) Two musical terms which indicate that a song is to be sung brightly.
   (c) Two musical terms which indicate that a song is to be sung sadly.
5. Write a melody starting on *so* to the following rhythm:

MELODIES

The songs and themes that follow will serve as a review of the work covered so far. Some of them present difficulties, but you should be able to master them before proceeding further.

Downton

Hymn

Orlando Gibbons

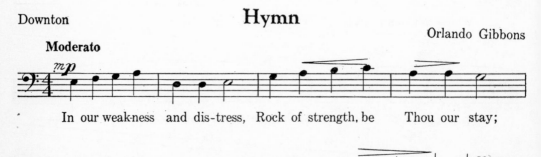

48

Good-night to You All

Con brio

Old Round

Good - night to you all and sweet be your
sleep; May an - gels a - round you their sweet vi - gils
keep. Good - night, good - night, good - night, good - night.

How Can I Leave Thee?
(Adapted)

Thuringian Folk Song

Andante

How can I leave thee? How can I bear to part?
That thou hast all my heart, Dear - est, be - lieve.
Thou hast this soul of mine; So whol - ly it is thine
That I can love no one But thee a - lone.

49

Theme from the Piano Concerto

NOTE.—This melody is not as hard to sing as it may appear. Notice how the same rhythmic pattern is repeated throughout several bars. This is called a *sequence*.

Mozart

Allegretto

Welsh Hymn

Palgrave

Andante

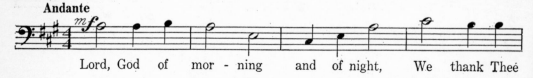

Lord, God of mor - ning and of night, We thank Thee

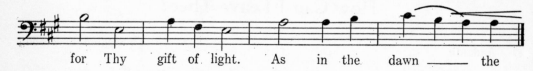

for Thy gift of light. As in the dawn —— the

sha - dows fly, We — seem to find Thee now more nigh.

Morning Praise

Beethoven

Andante

Love is to hu-man hearts what sun-shine is to flow'rs; And

friend-ship is the fair - est thing in this great world of ours.

Theme adapted from the Trio in E♭

Mozart

Allegretto

Theme adapted from the Clarinet Quintet

Mozart

Allegro

Theme from "Pictures at an Exhibition"

Moussorgsky

Grandioso

rall.

Waltz Theme

Tempo di valse

Johann Strauss

Thou Fillest My Heart

German

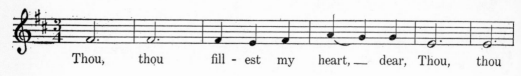

Thou, thou fill - est my heart, — dear, Thou, thou

plea - sest mine eye. Thou, thou troub-lest me sore - ly,

Know'st not how faith - ful am I? ____ Ah yes,

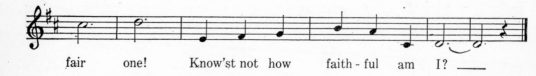

fair one! Know'st not how faith - ful am I? ____

SECTION TWO

Chapter 8

HALF NOTE AND EIGHTH NOTE BEAT VALUES

Half Note Beat Values

You learned on page 7 that the upper figure of a time signature tells the number of beats in a bar, and the lower the value of the beat. Thus in $\frac{2}{4}$, $\frac{3}{4}$, $\frac{4}{4}$ time each beat receives the value of a quarter note. It is also possible to use the half note as the beat value, in which case the time signatures will become $\frac{2}{2}$, $\frac{3}{2}$, $\frac{4}{2}$. The half note ♩ now receives one beat, and the whole note o now receives two beats. If we wish four beats, we may either tie two whole notes o⌢o or use a note called a *breve* written thus: ‖o‖, which has double the value of a whole note.

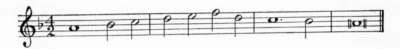

If you compare the above example with this:

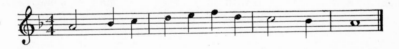

you will see that there is actually no difference in the sound of the two of them. The half note time signatures, therefore, tell us nothing new and we could well do without them, but since they are still used in a great deal of church and folk music, it is necessary to become acquainted with them. Note that the sign ¢ is frequently used for $\frac{2}{2}$. (Compare C and $\frac{4}{4}$, page 15.)

WRITTEN EXERCISES

1. Re-write the following in $\frac{4}{4}$ time:

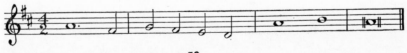

53

2. Re-write the following in ¾ time:

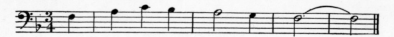

3. Re-write the following in ¢ time:

A Familiar Tune

O come, all ye faith - ful, Joy - ful and tri . - um - phant

Let Us With a Gladsome Mind

John Milton   Arthur Sullivan

Sostenuto

Let   us   with   a   glad - some   mind

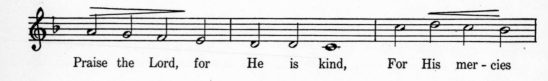

Praise the Lord, for He is kind, For His mer - cies

shall en - dure, E - ver faith - ful, e - ver sure.

From Thee All Skill and Science Flow

Charles Kingsley

Crüger (17th Century)

From Thee all skill and sci - ence flow,

All pi - ty, care, and love, All calm and

cou - rage, faith, and hope. Oh! Pour them from a - bove.

The Bee

NOTE. This may be sung as a round. The figures 1, 2, 3 indicate the points at which the various voices enter.

Old English Round

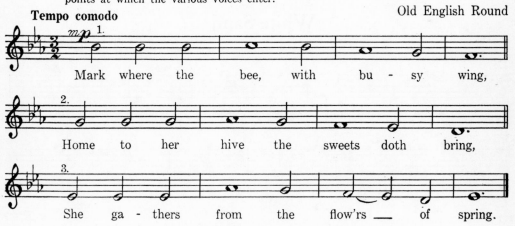

Mark where the bee, with bu - sy wing,

Home to her hive the sweets doth bring,

She ga - thers from the flow'rs __ of spring.

Old Welsh Tune

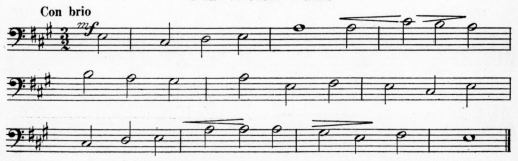

Fill Thou My Life

Bonar

Handel

Fill Thou my life, O Lord my God, in e - v'ry part with praise, —— That my whole be - ing may pro - claim Thy Be - ing and Thy ways. ——

White Sand

Old English Round

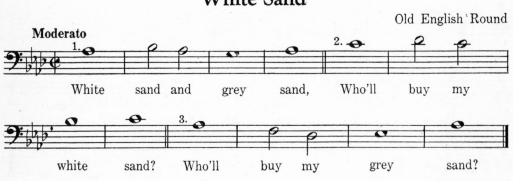

White sand and grey sand, Who'll buy my white sand? Who'll buy my grey sand?

Theme from the "Leonore Overture No. 3"

Beethoven

The Eighth Note and Eighth Rest

The eighth note, written ♪ or ♩, receives, as its name suggests, one eighth the value of a whole note.   The eighth rest is written thus: ϟ.   If we consider the eighth note to be the beat value, we get three more time signatures: $\frac{4}{8}$, $\frac{3}{8}$, and $\frac{2}{8}$.   The values of the various notes and rests in beats will now be:

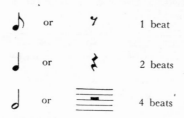

♪	or ϟ	1 beat
♩	or ξ	2 beats
♩	or ▬	4 beats

$\frac{3}{8}$ time is the only one of these three time signatures that is commonly used to-day.

Barred Eighth Note

When two or more eighth notes are sung to one word syllable, they are not only slurred but are also joined by lines which replace the tails; *i.e.* ♪ ♪ becomes ♫ , etc.   These lines are also employed to show the grouping of eighth notes in instrumental music.   Note that when several eighth notes are grouped, it is not possible to follow the rules regarding the position of the stems (see page 6).

Let all men sing this day

WRITTEN EXERCISES

1. Re-write the following in $\frac{3}{4}$ time:

2. Re-write the following in $\frac{4}{8}$ time:

57

The Manger

Austrian Carol

Moderato

With - in ___ a sta - ble low - - -
His bed ___ a hum - ble man - - -

ly, there lies a Babe ___ di - vine, ___
ger 'midst won - d'ring ass and kine. ___

This bles - séd Babe di - vine. ___

Minuet

Pleyel

Tempo giusto

Un Flambeau

Translated by
Ann Trimingham

Old French Carol

Giocoso

Bring a torch, ___ Jean - nette, Is - a - bel - la, Bring a
Un flam - beau, ___ Jean - nette, Is - a - bell - e, un flam -

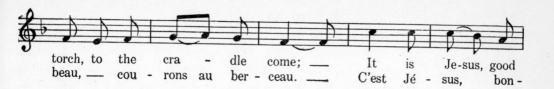

torch, to the cra - dle come; — It is Je-sus, good
beau, — cou - rons au ber - ceau. — C'est Jé - sus, bon -

friends of the vil - lage, Je - sus is born, and Ma - ry
nes gens du ha - meau, Le Christ est né, Ma - rie ap -

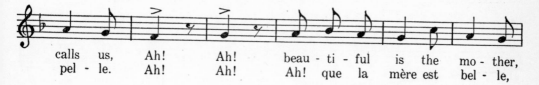

calls us, Ah! Ah! beau - ti - ful is the mo - ther,
pel - le. Ah! Ah! Ah! que la mère est bel - le,

Ah! Ah! beau - ti - ful is her Son! —
Ah! Ah! Ah! que l'en - fant est beau! —

From *The Silver Book of Songs*, used by permission of Hall & McCreary Company, Chicago, and Gordon V. Thompson Limited, Toronto.

Melody

Beethoven

Andante

Disregard of Time Signature

Frequently, for the purpose of satisfactory performance, the instruction of the time signature may be disregarded. For instance, if a melody in $\frac{4}{4}$ time is to be sung at a very slow tempo, the conductor may find it more convenient to count eight beats to the bar, each note receiving double its value in beats.

Observe and sing the following:

Chorale

Music in fast $\frac{3}{4}$ time often receives one beat to the bar, in which case, the accent on the third beat (see page 34) generally disappears.

Oh, How Lovely is the Evening!

Old English Round

Gai lon la, gai le rosier

French Canadian Folk Song

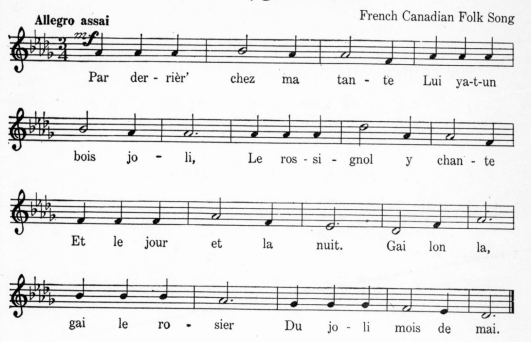

Allegro assai

Par der - rièr' chez ma tan - te Lui ya-t-un
bois jo - li, Le ros - si - gnol y chan - te
Et le jour et la nuit. Gai lon la,
gai le ro - sier Du jo - li mois de mai.

From *Chansons Populaires du Canada* by Ernest Gagnon, used by permission of Librairie Beauchemin Limitée, Montreal.

Theme from the Fifth Symphony

NOTE.—The sign  indicates that the previous bar is to be repeated.

Scherzo

Beethoven

Chapter 9

THE EIGHTH NOTE AND REST WITH HALF BEAT VALUE

In $\frac{3}{8}$, $\frac{4}{8}$, and $\frac{2}{8}$ time the eighth note receives one beat. If the eighth note is used in $\frac{4}{4}$, $\frac{3}{4}$, or $\frac{2}{4}$ time, it receives only one half a beat. Reading two notes to the beat requires some care at first. Observe the following exercises.

PRELIMINARY VOCAL EXERCISE

A Familiar Tune

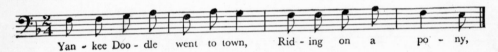

Yan - kee Doo - dle went to town, Rid - ing on a po - ny,

D'où viens-tu, bergère?

French Canadian Folk Carol

Con espressione

"D'où viens - tu, ber - gè - re, D'où viens - tu?"

"Je viens de l'é - ta - ble De m'y pro - me - ner;

J'ai vu un mi - ra - cle Ce soir ar - ri vé."

From *Chansons Populaires du Canada* by Ernest Gagnon, used by permission of Librairie Beauchemin Limitée, Montreal.

Old English Carol

Andante

A — vir - gin most— ho - ly, the — pro - phet fore -
told, Should bring us a — Sa - viour which now— we be -
hold, To — be our Re - deem - er from e - vil and
sin, Which A-dam's trans - gres-sion had wrap - péd us in.

The Twenty-Third Psalm

Havergal

Andante

The Lord's my Shep - herd, I'll not want: He
makes me down to lie, In pas-tures green; He
lea - deth me the qui - et wa - ters by.

Admiral's Song

From "H.M.S. Pinafore"

Gilbert

Sullivan

Marcato

His nose should pant, and his lip should curl, His
His foot should stamp, and his throat should growl, His

cheek should flame, and his brow should furl, His bosom should heave, and his
hair should twirl, and his face should scowl, His eyes should flash and his

heart should glow, And his fist be ev-er read-y for a knock-down blow.
breast pro-trude, And __ this should, be his custom-ar-y at-ti-tude.

Spinning Song

Allegretto

German Folk Song

"Spin, spin, O my dar-ling daugh-ter, I'll buy thee some
"Spin, spin, I will buy, my daugh-ter, A hus-band for

shoes." "Yes, yes, Mo-ther, dear-est Mo-ther, With buck-les on the
thee!" "Yes, yes, Mo-ther, dear-est Mo-ther, 'Twill just do for __

toes! I can't go on spin.-ning, My fin-ger is
me! I'll now go on spin-ning, My fin-ger's stopped

smart-ing And feels, and feels, and feels ve-ry sore!"
smart-ing And hurts, and hurts, and hurts me no more!"

From *Songs of Germany* by Max Spicker, English translation by H. G. Chapman. Copyright, 1904, by G. Schirmer, Inc. Copyright renewal assigned, 1932, to G. Schirmer, Inc.

Song of the Exile

Irish Folk Song

Dolce

Far, far a-way from friends — and home, In sorrow bowed and

weep - ing sore, Through dis-tant lands I sad - ly

roam, Where e-v'ry house has barred —— its door.

Theme from the Horn Sextet in F

Mozart

Allegro marcato

The Young Heir

Old English

From "Pills to Purge Melancholy" (1699)

Con spirito

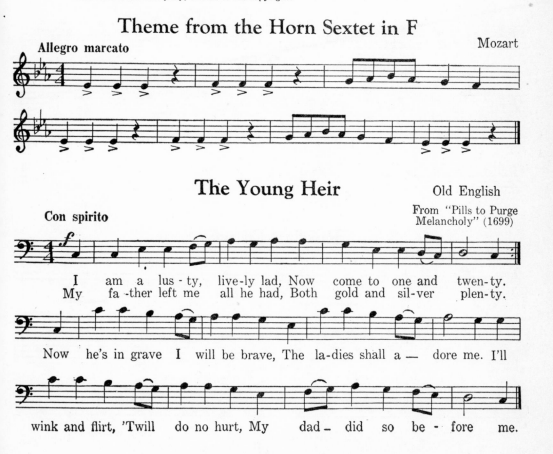

I am a lus - ty, live-ly lad, Now come to one and twen-ty.
My fa-ther left me all he had, Both gold and sil-ver plen-ty.

Now he's in grave I will be brave, The la-dies shall a — dore me. I'll

wink and flirt, 'Twill do no hurt, My dad — did so be - fore me.

Minuet from the Tenth Concerto

Grazioso

Corelli

Robin Hood

Con brio

Old English Ballad

In sum - mer time when leaves grow green, and

flow'rs are fresh and gay, Bold Ro - bin _ Hood and his

mer-ry, mer-ry men were dis - pos - ed to play.

Russian Dance

Allegro con forza

Theme from "Espana"

NOTE. In the following melody there is a repeat. Note, however, that the last bar differs each time. The first and second endings are indicated by the signs *1st* and *2nd*.

Chabrier

Note the time signatures of the following melodies. The quarter note here will receive the time value that the eighth note does in $\frac{2}{4}$ time.

Chorale from the Christmas Oratorio

J. S. Bach

How shall I fit-ly meet Thee, And give Thee wel-come due?
The na-tions long to greet Thee, And I would greet Thee, too.

O Fount of Light, shine bright-ly u-pon my darken'd heart, That

I — may serve Thee right-ly, And know Thee as Thou art.

Ye Watchers and Ye Holy Ones

17th Century Melody

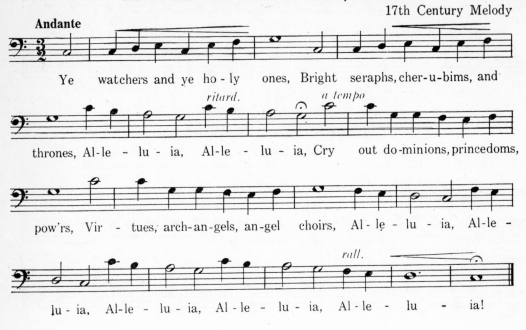

Ye watchers and ye ho-ly ones, Bright seraphs, cher-u-bims, and thrones, Al-le-lu-ia, Al-le-lu-ia, Cry out do-minions, princedoms, pow'rs, Vir-tues, arch-an-gels, an-gel choirs, Al-le-lu-ia, Al-le-lu-ia, Al-le-lu-ia, Al-le-lu-ia, Al-le-lu-ia!

God Rest You Merry, Gentlemen

Old English Carol

God rest you mer-ry, gen-tle-men, Let no-thing you dis-may. Re-mem-ber Christ our Sa-viour Was born on Christ-mas Day, To save us all from Sa-tan's pow'r, When we were gone a-stray.

The Little Man

Allegro con brio

Russian Folk Song

There was a lit - tle man with a great big bas - ket Who did start out one day for the fair. ___ He had a hun-dred rub- les in his well - stuff'd purse, But he spent not a one when he got there. ___

In the following melodies the eighth rest appears on the second half of the beat. Be sure to cut the eighth note short enough.

Dutch Dance Tune

Marcato

Theme from the String Quartet in E♭

Haydn
(Op. 33, No. 2)

Tempo di minuetto

Rhenish Dance Tune

Con spirito

Old French Gavotte

From Time of Louis XIV

Con moto e marcato

WRITTEN EXERCISES

1. Write a passage of four bars containing examples of ♪, ♫ and 𝄾.

2. Rewrite the same passage in ¢ time.

Chapter 10

THE DOTTED QUARTER NOTE. THE EIGHTH REST (Continued)

The Dotted Quarter Note

Review page 30. There you learned that the dot after a note increases that note's time value by one-half. In $\frac{2}{4}$, $\frac{3}{4}$, or $\frac{4}{4}$ time, therefore, the dotted quarter note or rest will receive one and one half beats. The dotted quarter note followed by an eighth note is a common rhythm. The same rhythm is produced if a quarter note is tied to an eighth note.

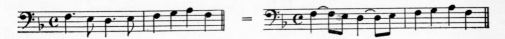

WRITTEN EXERCISES

1. Change the rhythm of the following, dotting the rest and at least two of the quarter notes:

2. Write four or eight bars of music containing examples of the dotted half note and the dotted quarter note.

PRELIMINARY VOCAL EXERCISE

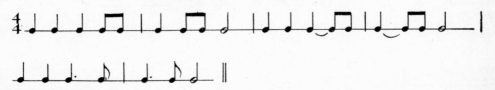

A Familiar Tune

Can you name it?

71

Sovereign Ruler of the Skies

Ryland
Pleyel

Moderato

Sov'-reign ru - ler   of the skies,   E - ver gra-cious,   e - ver wise,

All our times   are   in Thy hand,   All e-vents at   Thy command.

Sir John Franklin

J. Murray Gibbon
Sea Shanty

Allegro

Oh,   Frank-lin crossed the   Bar-ren Lands a - long   the Cop-per-

mine   To   find the North-West   Pas - sage, for his   thoughts did so in -

cline, —   Sing-ing, "Blow, ye winds of the   North Pole, Blow, ye winds, hi-

ho!   Blow a-way the   po-lar night,   Blow, ye winds, hi   - ho!"

From *New World Ballads* by John Murray Gibbon, used by permission of the author and the publisher, Gordon V. Thompson Limited.

Io Vivat

Dutch Folk Tune

Theme from the Symphony in C Major

Schubert

Theme from the String Quartet in F

Brahms
(Op. 88)

March of King James II

NOTE.—*The Dancing Master* was a book of tunes which was very popular in England during the later 17th century.

From "The Dancing Master"

Theme from the Impromptu

Schubert

Thanksgiving Hymn

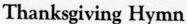

Gordon V. Thompson

Old Netherlands Folk Song

Maestoso

We thank Thee, our Fa - ther, for all Thou pro - vid - est, For

win - ter, for spring, and for sum - mer and fall; For

rain and for sun-shine, the gift of Thy _ good-ness, We

rall.

sing in a - dor - a - tion and thank Thee for all.

From *The Silver Book of Songs*, used by permission of the publisher, Gordon V. Thompson Limited.

Nocturne from "A Midsummer Night's Dream"

Mendelssohn

Dolce

Theme adapted from the Haffner Symphony

Mozart

Tempo di minuetto

Fine

D.C. al Fine

Note the sound of the dotted half note in ¢ time and of the dotted quarter note in ⅜ time.

Theme adapted from "The Marriage of Figaro"

Mozart

Presto con forza

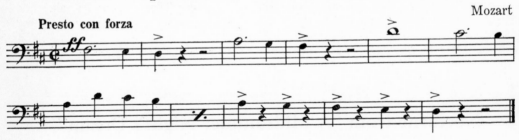

Blue Waves Are Tossing

From Matthew Arnold

Bohemian Folk Song

Moderato

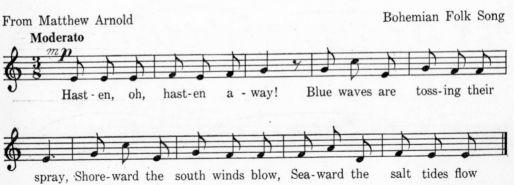

Hast-en, oh, hast-en a - way! Blue waves are toss-ing their

spray, Shore-ward the south winds blow, Sea-ward the salt tides flow

76

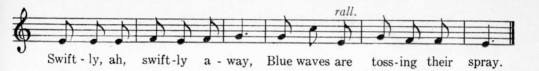

Swift - ly, ah, swift-ly a - way, Blue waves are toss-ing their spray.

Eighth Rests

In the following, the eighth rest appears on the beat. Note that the rhythmic form ♩ 𝄽 ♪ is the same as ♩. ♪ except that a rest replaces a dot.

The Monotone

Cornelius

I hear a tone so wondrous rare, It fills my

heart, 'tis e - ver there. ___ Ah, can it be the last faint

breath That stirr'd thy pal- lid lips ere death?___ Is it the

ten-der mon - o - tone Of church bell which for thee made moan?

Lo, still it comes so full, so clear, As though thy

soul were float - ing near, ___ As though with

love and yearn-ing deep, You sang my bit-ter pain to sleep.

Dans tous les cantons

French Canadian Folk Song

Allegretto

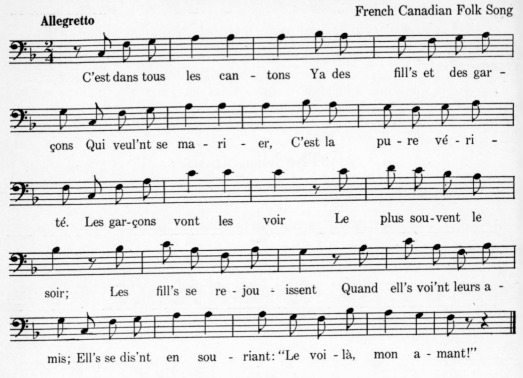

C'est dans tous les can - tons Y a des fill's et des gar - çons Qui veul'nt se ma - ri - er, C'est la pu - re vé - ri - té. Les gar - çons vont les voir Le plus sou - vent le soir; Les fill's se re - jou - issent Quand ell's voi'nt leurs a - mis; Ell's se dis'nt en sou - riant: "Le voi - là, mon a - mant!"

From *Chansons Populaires du Canada* by Ernest Gagnon, used by permission of Librairie Beauchemin Limitée, Montreal.

The Massacre of the Macpherson

W. E. Aytoun

Con spirito

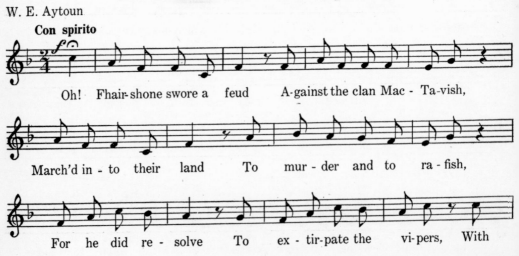

Oh! Fhair-shone swore a feud A-gainst the clan Mac - Ta-vish, March'd in - to their land To mur - der and to ra - fish, For he did re - solve To ex - tir-pate the vi-pers, With

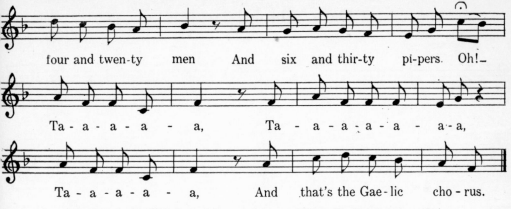

four and twen-ty men And six and thir-ty pi-pers. Oh!—

Ta - a - a - a - a, Ta - a - a - a - a - a - a,

Ta - a - a - a - a, And that's the Gae-lic cho-rus.

From *Bon Gaultier Ballads*, used by permission of William Blackwood & Sons, Ltd. Edinburgh.

King Arthur Had Three Sons

Tempo giusto

English Folk Song

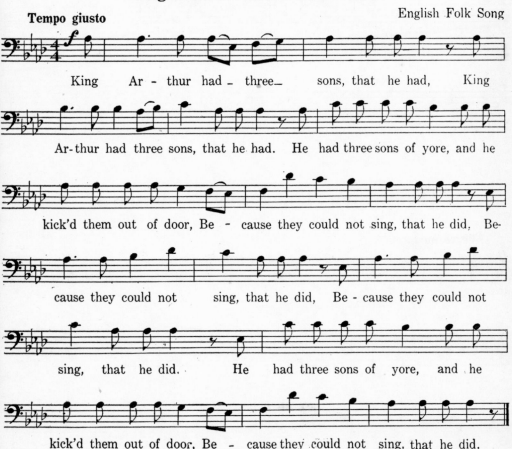

King Ar - thur had — three— sons, that he had, King

Ar-thur had three sons, that he had. He had three sons of yore, and he

kick'd them out of door, Be - cause they could not sing, that he did, Be-

cause they could not sing, that he did, Be - cause they could not

sing, that he did. He had three sons of yore, and he

kick'd them out of door, Be - cause they could not sing, that he did.

Hola!

German Folk Tune

Allegro

Come all ye lus - ty gal - lants and
The moon shines o'er the stee - ple, we'll

join the hap - py throng. Be mer - ry, be mer - ry, we'll
dance the whole night long. Be mer - ry, be mer - ry, we'll

dance and gai- ly sing. Ho - la, ho - la, ho - la, ho -
make the wel-kin ring.

la, ho - la, ho - la, ho - la, ho - la!

Theme from "Eine Kleine Nachtmusik"

NOTE.—The title of this composition means "A Little Night Music."

Mozart

Allegro moderato

Theme from the First Symphony

Allegro

Beethoven

Note the value of the quarter rest in the following:

O Tempora! O Mores!

Old College Song

Allegro giocoso

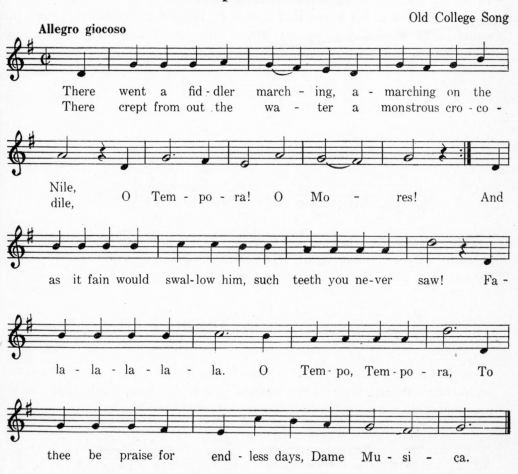

There went a fid - dler march - ing, a - marching on the
There crept from out the wa - ter a monstrous cro - co -

Nile,
dile, O Tem - po - ra! O Mo - res! And

as it fain would swal-low him, such teeth you ne-ver saw! Fa -

la - la - la - la - la. O Tem - po, Tem - po - ra, To

thee be praise for end - less days, Dame Mu - si - ca.

Chapter 11

SHARPS, FLATS, AND NATURALS

Accidentals

Review pages 5 and 6. There you learned the use of flats and sharps in helping to find *do* or the keynote. Examine the piano keyboard again (page 2). The distance from the note C to the note D is called a *tone*. If you strike the black key between them, you will find that it produces a sound half-way between C and D. This distance from C or from D to the black key is called a *semitone*. In music, a sharp before a note indicates that it is to be raised a semitone, and a flat before a note shows that it is to be lowered a semitone. Hence the sound of the black key mentioned above may be indicated in two ways as shown below.

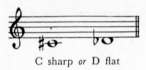

C sharp *or* D flat

Similarly, the following pairs of notes have the same sound:

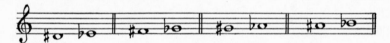

There is no black key on the keyboard between E and F, because these notes are only a semitone apart. The same thing applies to B and C. Hence the following pairs of notes have the same sound:

Sharps and flats used in front of notes to alter their normal sound are called *accidentals*. When a sharp or flat is placed in front of a note, it affects all following notes of the same pitch *until the end of the bar* has been reached.

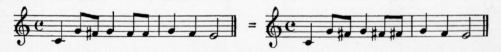

82

The Natural Sign

To restore a sharpened or flattened note to its original form *before* the end of the bar, a **natural** sign, ♮, is used. Frequently, for safety's sake, the natural sign is employed even *after* the end of the bar.

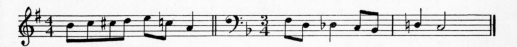

When a note is sharpened, the vowel sound of its solfa name is changed to *i: do* sharpened becomes *di, re* sharpened becomes *ri,* etc. When it is flattened, the vowel sound is changed to *a; mi* flattened becomes *ma, re* flattened becomes *ra,* etc.

WRITTEN EXERCISE

Re-write the following correctly:

PRELIMINARY VOCAL EXERCISES

1.

2.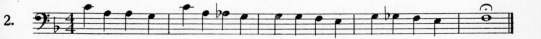

Impromptu

Schubert

Night Song

Moderato

Beethoven

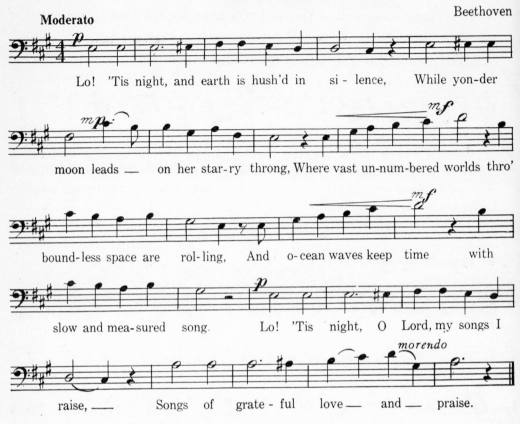

Lo! 'Tis night, and earth is hush'd in si - lence, While yon-der

moon leads — on her star-ry throng, Where vast un-num-bered worlds thro'

bound-less space are rol-ling, And o-cean waves keep time with

slow and mea-sured song. Lo! 'Tis night, O Lord, my songs I

raise, — Songs of grate - ful love — and — praise.

Theme from the Eighth Symphony

Beethoven

Allegretto

Musette adapted from "Armide"

NOTE.—A musette is a graceful dance, very similar to the gavotte.

Gluck

Grazioso

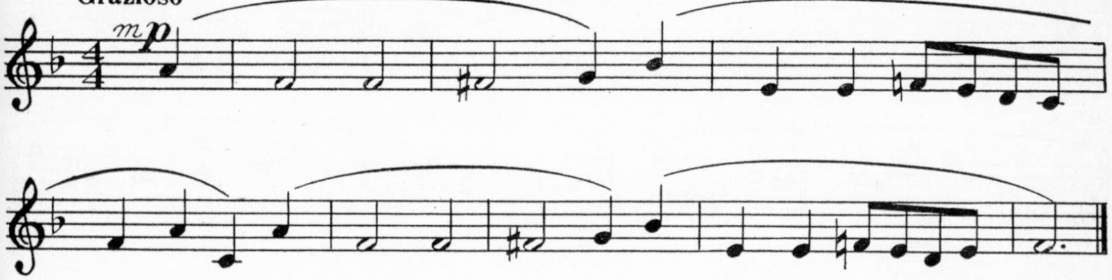

Theme adapted from the String Quartet in B♭

Tempo di minuetto

Haydn

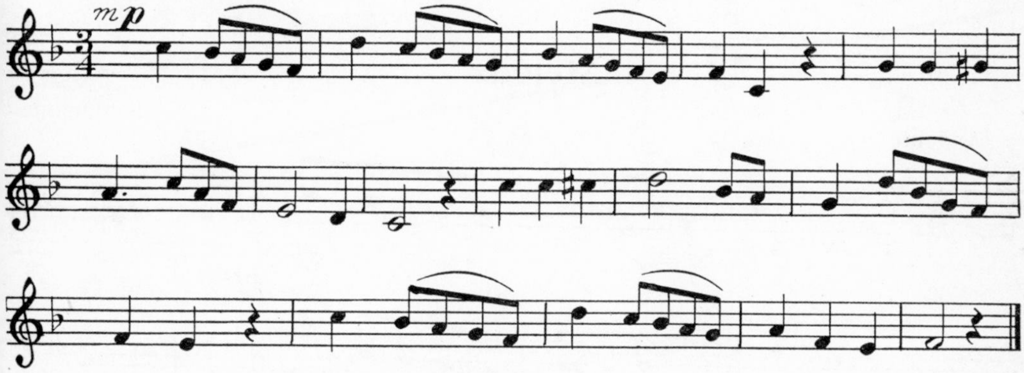

Melody

Mozart

Tranquillo

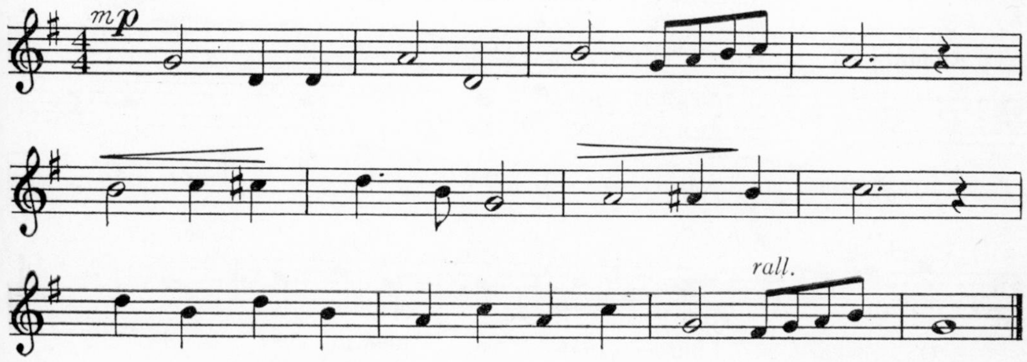

Theme from Overture to "A Midsummer Night's Dream"

Mendelssohn

Con passione

Melody

Schumann

Andante

Excerpt from "Lohengrin"

Wagner

Andante

Dost thou not breathe, as I, the scent of flow - ers?

O — what e - mo - tions on their in - cense roll!

Theme from the Piano Concerto in A Minor

Schumann

Con tenerezza

Theme from "Ruy Blas"

Mendelssohn

Tempo giusto

Theme from the String Sextet in B♭

Brahms

Allegro ma non troppo

Chapter 12

MAJOR SCALES. MODULATION TO THE DOMINANT

The Scale of C Major

A series of notes rising or falling in some sort of regular order is called a *scale.*   There are actually hundreds of different scales used by the various peoples of the world, but the one most familiar to our ears is the *major scale,* which we can hear by playing the white notes on the piano from C to C.   A great number of our songs are based on the major scale.   This is illustrated in such tunes as *The Bluebells of Scotland* or the following:

Joy to the world, the Lord is come!

The above scale is the *scale of C major,* and the tune is said to be in the **key of C major.**

The Scale of G Major

You have already learn-
ed that some of the white
keys of the piano are a tone
apart and some a semitone
apart (see page 82). By ex-
amining the keyboard you
will see that the scale of C
follows this definite pattern of
tones and semitones: Tone,
Tone, Semitone, Tone, Tone,
Tone, Semitone.

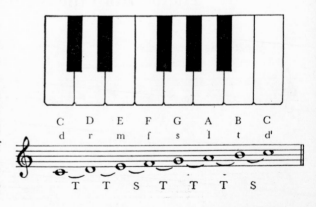

This is the proper pattern for all major scales and the one our ear is used to.

Suppose you play another scale of white notes from G to G. This is not a true major scale, and its effect is unsatisfactory because its tones and semitones are not in proper order, *i.e.* T T S T T S T instead of T T S T T T S. If, however, you sharpen the F, you will get a satisfactory scale.

T   T   S   T   T   S   T   T   T   S   T   T   T   S

You are now in the **key of G,** and all music in the key of G must use sharpened F's. This fact is indicated by placing an F# at the beginning of the music, thus creating a key signature (see page 5). Since the key signature indicates that F's are to be sharpened, it is not necessary to place them throughout the music.

Solfa and Technical Names

You will see presently that it is possible to build a major scale starting on any note. As you move about, the order of the alphabetical names will vary, but the tonic solfa names move with the scale and will always be the same; *e.g.*

Scale of C: C D E F G A B C—d r m f s l t d¹
Scale of G: G A B C D E F# G—d r m f s l t d¹

This is why solfa syllables are so useful, for if you can read with them in one key, you can read with them in any key. Each note of the major scale has a **technical name,** which, like the solfa names moves with the key. These names are sometimes abbreviated in the form of Roman numerals.

	SOLFA NAME	TECHNICAL NAME	ABBREVIATION
8th note of the scale	*do¹*	Tonic (upper)	I
7th note of the scale	*ti*	Leading Note	VII
6th note of the scale	*la*	Submediant	VI
5th note of the scale	*so*	Dominant	V
4th note of the scale	*fa*	Subdominant	IV
3rd note of the scale	*mi*	Mediant	III
2nd note of the scale	*re*	Supertonic	II
1st note of the scale	*do*	Tonic (lower)	I

When you constructed the scale of G, you were actually building the scale starting on the dominant of the scale of C. If you now build a scale on the dominant of G, you will produce the scale of **D major** and in doing so, will find

it necessary to sharpen both F and C. The key signature now becomes .

Moving next to the dominant of D and so on in the same manner, you can eventually construct a whole series of scales with key signatures as follows:

key of G key of D key of A key of E key of B key of F♯ key of C♯

The following points will help you to remember these keys and key signatures:

1. Each key is the dominant of the one preceding it.
2. Each key signature adds one sharp to the key signature preceding it.
3. The newly sharpened note in each case is always the leading note of the key or *ti* (compare page 5). The last two scales in the above example start on sharpened notes. Why?

WRITTEN EXERCISES

1. Write, in both treble and bass clefs, the scales of all the keys listed in the example above.
2. Write the key signatures of the following scales:

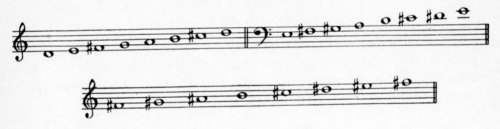

3. On what notes do each of the following appear?
    (*a*) the dominant of D major (*c*) the supertonic of A major
    (*b*) the mediant of E major (*d*) the leading note of F♯ major

Modulation and the Shifting Do

The key signature tells what key a tune is in, but very frequently a melody disregards the signature and moves into another key. Note the following:

This tune starts in C major, but by the second and third bars it has moved into G major. You can tell this by the presence of the F sharps and by the

90

portion of the G major scale which appears in bar 2.   If you are alert, you can also "feel" the new key as you sing.   The ability to sense changes of key and to feel their *tonality,* as it is called, will come with practice and is very important for success in sight singing.   In using tonic solfa, you may, if you wish, keep the syllables belonging to C major and sing *fi* for F♯ (see Chapter 11).   Since, however, the syllables change with the key, it would be more logical to shift the *do* to G instead of C.   The above diagram illustrates the two ways of reading the passage.   You may use either, but in cases where the new key lasts for some time, it is better to shift the *do.*   The exact point at which the shift to *do* is made is not always clear.   Careful practice, however, will help you to feel it.

The process of changing key in a song is called *modulation.*   All the following melodies modulate to the dominant of their key.   Name the new keys in each case.

A Familiar Tune

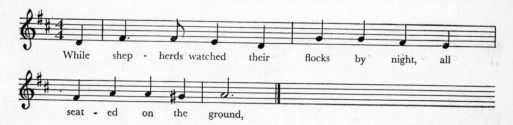

While shep - herds watched their flocks by night, all seat - ed on the ground,

Danish Folk Dance

Allegro marcato

Fine

D.C. al Fine

91

The Dear Little Shamrock

Irish Folk Song

Moderato

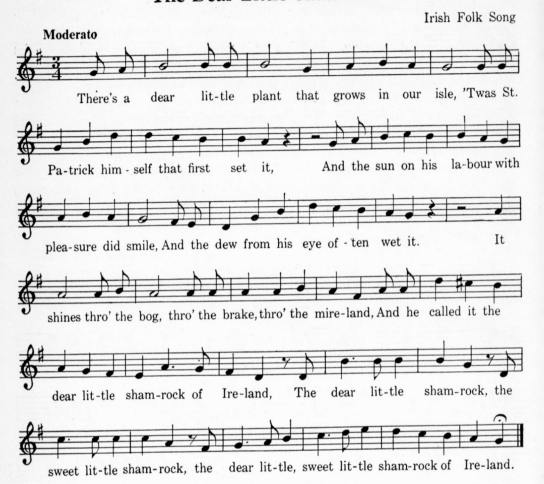

There's a dear lit-tle plant that grows in our isle, 'Twas St.

Pa-trick him - self that first set it, And the sun on his la-bour with

plea-sure did smile, And the dew from his eye of - ten wet it. It

shines thro' the bog, thro' the brake, thro' the mire-land, And he called it the

dear lit-tle sham-rock of Ire-land, The dear lit-tle sham-rock, the

sweet lit-tle sham-rock, the dear lit-tle, sweet lit-tle sham-rock of Ire-land.

Czech Folk Dance

Allegro moderato

Excerpt from the "Ave Verum"

Translated by F. D. Roy

Mozart

Adagio

A - ve, a - ve ve - rum cor - pus na - tum
Je - sus our Sa - viour born of Mar - y, Thy poor

de Ma - ri - a vir - gi - ne, ve - re pas sum
bo - dy bro - ken for our sake! We ex - toll Thee

im - mo - la - tum in cru - ce pro ho - mi - ne.
cru - ci - fied on the cru - el Cross to save us all.

He is an Englishman!

Gilbert

From "H.M.S. Pinafore"

Sullivan

Maestoso

For — he him-self has said it, And it's great-ly to his

cre - dit That he is an Eng-lish-man! That he is an Eng-lish -

man, For he might have been a Roos-ian, A French, or Turk, or

Proo-sian, Or per-haps I-tal - i - an, Or per-haps I-tal - i - an. But in

spite of all temp-ta - tions To be-long to o-ther na - tions, He re-

mains an Eng-lish-man! He re - mains an Eng - - - lish-man!

Marie Antoinette's Song

NOTE.—Marie Antoinette, like Henry VIII, was fond of music and tried her hand at composing.

Marie Antoinette

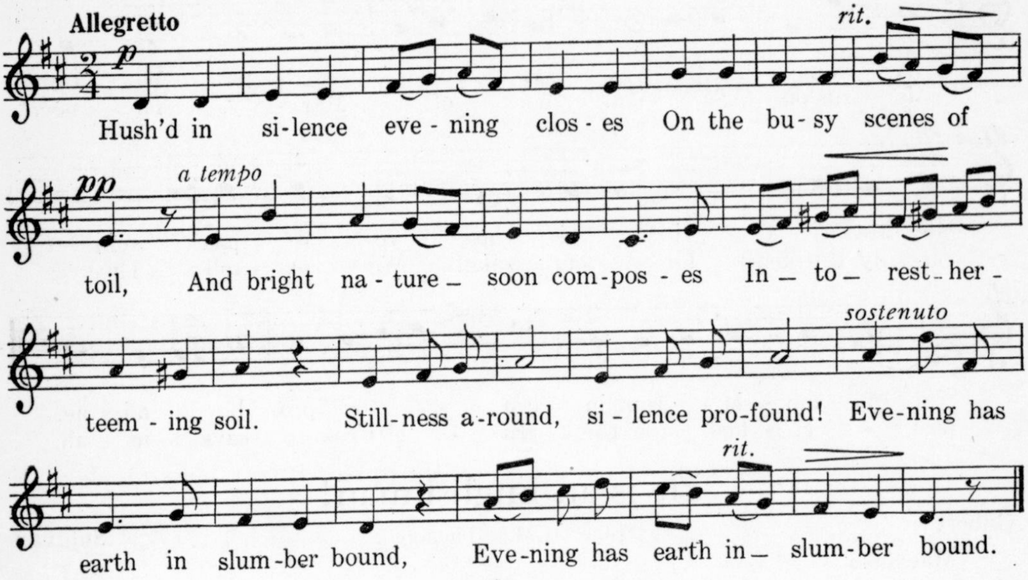
Allegretto
p
rit.
Hush'd in si-lence eve-ning clos-es On the bu-sy scenes of
pp
a tempo
toil, And bright na-ture_ soon com-pos-es In_ to_ rest_her-
teem-ing soil. Still-ness a-round, si-lence pro-found! Eve-ning has
sostenuto
earth in slum-ber bound, Eve-ning has earth in_ slum-ber bound.
rit.

Now is the Month of Maying

Morley

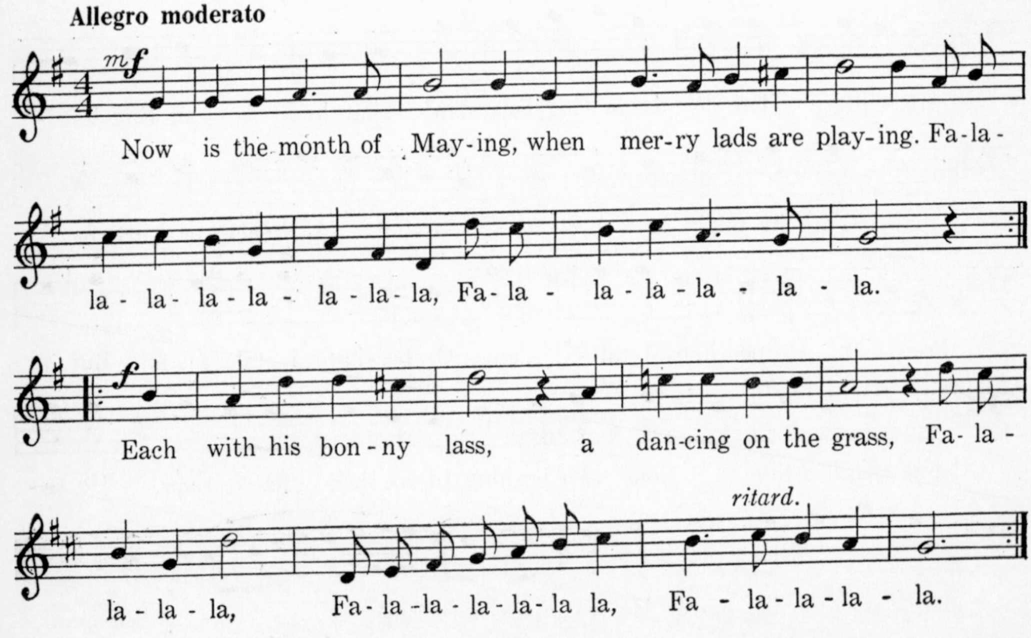
Allegro moderato
mf
Now is the month of May-ing, when mer-ry lads are play-ing. Fa-la-
la-la-la-la-la-la-la, Fa-la-la-la-la-la-la.
f
Each with his bon-ny lass, a dan-cing on the grass, Fa-la-
ritard.
la-la-la, Fa-la-la-la-la-la la, Fa-la-la-la-la.

Chapter 13

MAJOR SCALES (Continued). MODULATION TO THE SUBDOMINANT

Flat Scales

If you build a scale on the white keys starting with F, you get T T T S T T S. In order to preserve the proper order of tones and semitones for the major scale, you must flatten B. This gives a key signature with one flat.

The scale of F is built on the subdominant of C. If you build a scale on the subdominant of the scale of F, *i.e.* B♭, you get the key signature: . Proceeding the same way, you produce another series of scales with the following key signatures:

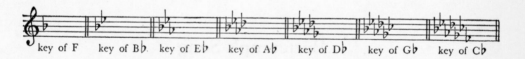

key of F   key of B♭   key of E♭   key of A♭   key of D♭   key of G♭   key of C♭

Note the following helpful points:
1. Each key is the subdominant of the key preceding it.
2. Each key signature adds one flat to the key signature preceding it.
3. The newly flattened note in each is always the subdominant (or *fa*) of the key (compare page 5).

Enharmonic Change

It is interesting to note that certain of the sharp and flat scales actually sound the same.

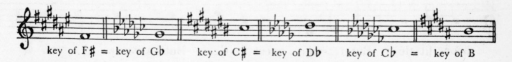

key of F♯ = key of G♭   key of C♯ = key of D♭   key of C♭ = key of B

95

This practice of changing the appearance of music on paper without changing its actual sound is known as *enharmonic change.* (Compare page 82.)

WRITTEN EXERCISES

1. Write, in both treble and bass clefs, the scales of all the keys listed in the second example on page 95.
2. Write the key signatures of the following scales:

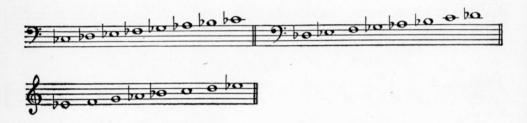

Modulation to the Subdominant

Some melodies modulate to the subdominant. Once again, it is generally better to shift *do.* Two ways of reading such a passage are illustrated.

Buttercup's Song

From "H.M.S. Pinafore"

Gilbert   Sullivan

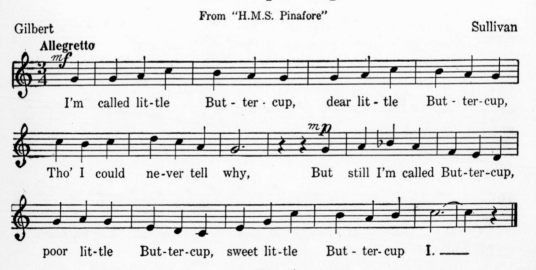

I'm called lit-tle But-ter-cup, dear lit-tle But-ter-cup,

Tho' I could ne-ver tell why, But still I'm called But-ter-cup,

poor lit-tle But-ter-cup, sweet lit-tle But-ter-cup I. ——

Passing By

From Ford's
"Music of Sundry Kinds"

Morey

There is a la - dye sweet and kind was

ne - ver face so pleased my mind; I did but see her

pass - ing by, and yet I love her till I die.

The Soldier's Farewell

Kinkel

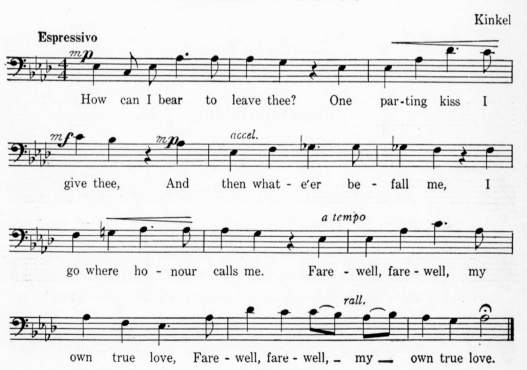

How can I bear to leave thee? One par - ting kiss I

give thee, And then what - e'er be - fall me, I

go where ho - nour calls me. Fare - well, fare - well, my

own true love, Fare - well, fare - well, _ my _ own true love.

One Morning in the Spring

Allegretto

Old English

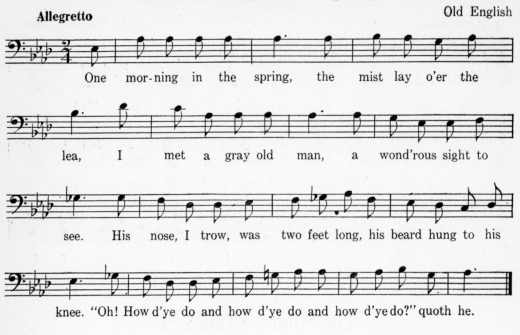

One mor-ning in the spring, the mist lay o'er the lea, I met a gray old man, a wond'rous sight to see. His nose, I trow, was two feet long, his beard hung to his knee. "Oh! How d'ye do and how d'ye do and how d'ye do?" quoth he.

Marching Song

Alla marcia

Russian Folk Song

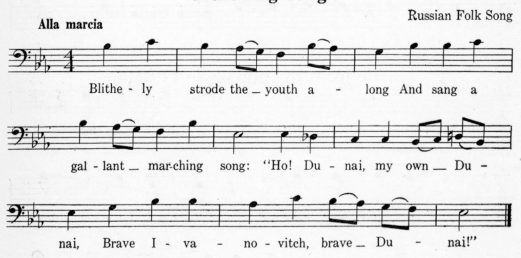

Blithe - ly strode the _ youth a - long And sang a gal - lant _ mar-ching song: "Ho! Du - nai, my own _ Du - nai, Brave I - va - no - vitch, brave _ Du - nai!"

From *Fifty Russian Folk Songs* by E. L. Swerkoff, English version by D. Millar Craig, used by permission of Novello & Company, Ltd., London.

The Faithful Sailor

Andantino

From "The Cobbler's Opera"

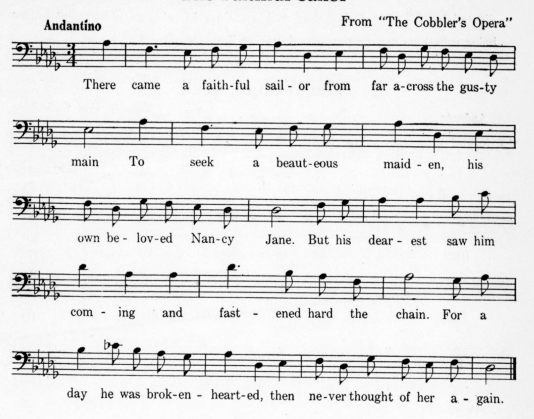

There came a faith-ful sail - or from far a-cross the gus-ty

main To seek a beaut-eous maid - en, his

own be - lov-ed Nan-cy Jane. But his dear - est saw him

com - ing and fast - ened hard the chain. For a

day he was brok-en - heart-ed, then ne-ver thought of her a - gain.

Theme from the Sonata in G Major

Beethoven

If a melody in a flat key modulates to the dominant, *fi* (or the new *ti*) is indicated by a ♮ sign rather than a sharp, since in this case a flattened note is being raised. Observe the following melodies:

The Wishing Well

Yugo-Slavian Folk Song

Through the dis-tant ver-dant for-est stands a wish-ing well, And
in the twi-light wist-ful lo-vers come to test its spell, Then
from its depths, — cool and frag-rant, comes the e-cho clear: — "Some
day, some day, the clouds will dis-ap-pear. Be
gay to-day, your hap-pi-ness is near."

Parting

Mendelssohn

The heav'n-ly coun-cil hath de-creed To try us, if we love in-deed, By
part-ing, Al-though 'twixt heav'n and earth there's naught So
bit-ter-ly with sor-row fraught As part-ing, Yes, part-ing.

From *Felix Mendelssohn Bartholdy's Songs* translated by Natalia Macfarren, used by permission of Novello & Company, Ltd., London.

Theme from "The Farewell Symphony"

Allegretto

Haydn

If a melody in a sharp key modulates to the subdominant, *ta* (or the new *fa*) is produced by a ♮ rather than a ♯ sign, since in this case, a sharpened note is being lowered.   Observe the following melodies:

Lead Us, Heavenly Father

Edmeston

Filitz

Sostenuto

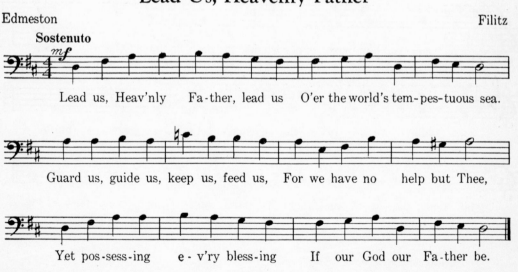

Lead us, Heav'nly   Fa-ther, lead us   O'er the world's tem-pes-tuous sea.

Guard us, guide us, keep us, feed us,   For we have no   help but Thee,

Yet pos-sess-ing   e - v'ry bless-ing   If   our God our   Fa-ther be.

101

Theme from the "Fantasia Impromptu"

Chopin

Tempo rubato

Excerpt from "Pique Dame"

Tschaikowsky

Dolce

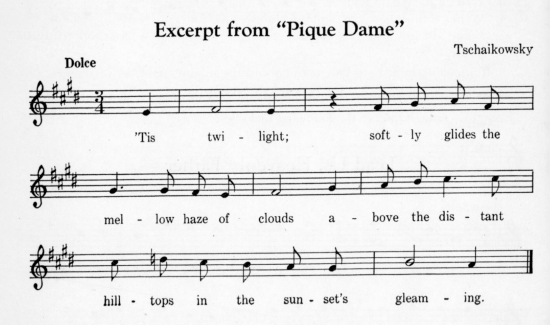

'Tis   twi - light;   soft - ly   glides the

mel - low haze of   clouds   a - bove the dis - tant

hill - tops   in   the   sun - set's   gleam - ing.

Chapter 14

REVIEW OF CHAPTERS 8-13

WRITTEN EXERCISES

1. Write a passage of at least four bars in $\frac{3}{4}$ time. Rewrite the same passage in $\frac{3}{2}$ time and in $\frac{3}{8}$ time.
2. Rewrite the following, substituting dots for ties wherever possible:

3. Write a melody of four bars in the key of A♭ major.
4. Write, with proper key signatures, the major scales of D, A♭, B, and F.
5. Write out any pair of scales that sound the same but appear differently on paper.

O Saviour Sweet

J. S. Bach

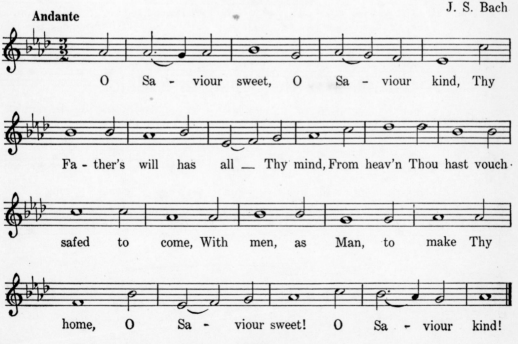

Andante

O Sa - viour sweet, O Sa - viour kind, Thy

Fa - ther's will has all — Thy mind, From heav'n Thou hast vouch·

safed to come, With men, as Man, to make Thy

home, O Sa - viour sweet! O Sa - viour kind!

Theme from the Violin Concerto in D

Beethoven

Andante

The Bailiff's Daughter

Old English Ballad

Moderato

There was a youth, and a well be-lo-ved youth, And— he was a squi-re's

son. He— loved the bai-liff's daugh-ter dear, That lived in — Is-ling-ton.

Theme from the Sonata in F Major

Beethoven

Allegretto

Song of the Western Men

Hawker

Cornish Song

Con energia

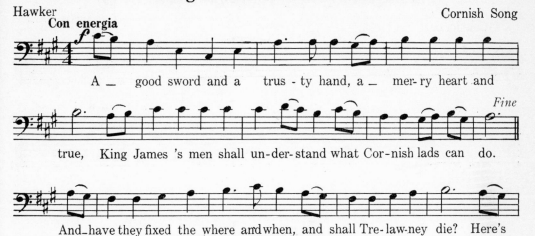

A — good sword and a trus-ty hand, a — mer-ry heart and

true, King James 's men shall un-der-stand what Cor-nish lads can do.

And—have they fixed the where and when, and shall Tre-law-ney die? Here's

twen-ty thou-sand Cor-nish men will — know the rea-son why.

The London Watchman

From *Songs of the British Islands*, Collected and Edited by Sir W. H. Hadow, By permission, from Curwen Edition No. 6179, published by J. Curwen & Sons, Ltd., 24 Berners Street, London, W.1.

NOTE.—A familiar sight in old London was the watchman who patrolled the streets announcing the time of night and the weather, and sometimes acting as a sort of policeman.

Andante

Old English

Past three o' - clock and a cold — fros-ty mor-ning; Past three o'-

clock, good mor-row mas-ters all! While in your beds you're peace-ful-ly

sleep-ing, Un-der — the — stars our watch we are keep-ing.

Theme from the Piano Concerto in B♭ Minor

Tschaikowsky

Hymn to Joy

From the Ninth Symphony

Beethoven

Hail thee, Joy, all hail, di - vin - est Daugh-ter of E -

lys - i - um. We ap-proach thy light so cheer-ing, to thy al - tar

now we come. Thou hast pow'r to bind to - ge - ther

what the world would rend a - part, And wher - e - ver thy

light wings flut - ter, love and peace are in my heart.

Oh No, John

Somerset Folk Song

Moderato

On yon-der hill there stands a — crea-ture, Who she is I do not know, I'll go — ask her hand in mar-riage. She must ans-wer

un poco ritard.

yes or no. "Oh no, John, no, John, no, John, no!"

The Wreath

Bayley

Old English Song

Espressivo

mp

Give thy wreath to me when the pe-tals die, —

Ne - ver let it be thrown ne - glect-ed by.

mf

Bloom and scent may per - ish, yet those leaves I'll cher-ish,

p

Hal-low'd — by thy touch; then give thy wreath to me.

I Love a Maiden Fair

Latin American Folk Song

Vivace

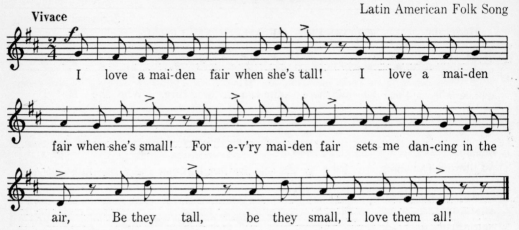

I love a mai-den fair when she's tall! I love a mai-den

fair when she's small! For e-v'ry mai-den fair sets me dan-cing in the

air, Be they tall, be they small, I love them all!

Theme adapted from the Piano Trio in G

Mozart

Tranquillo

My Little Queen

Brahms

Adagio

How art thou now, my lit-tle queen? May all de-

light, all joy be thine. — When thou dost smile, the scent of

dolce

spring Is round me blow-ing, Joy be thine, Joy be thine!

GLOSSARY OF MUSICAL TERMS

NOTE:

1. Abbreviated forms appear in brackets e.g., *Diminuendo (Dim.)*.

2. When two or more words mean the same thing, cross indexing is used; e.g., *Tempo primo* appears in alphabetical order and also along with *A tempo*.

Accelerando (Accel.), gradually increasing the speed.

Adagio, very slowly (see also *Grave* and *Largo*).

Ad libitum (Ad. lib.), A piacere, to be performed at the performer's pleasure, particularly as regards time.

Affetuoso, affectionately.

Agitato, in a restless or agitated manner.

Alla marcia, Marziale, in marching tempo.

Allargando, gradually broadening out in tone and tempo.

Allegro (Allᵒ), quickly and lively.

Amabile, in an agreeable manner.

Allegretto, a little less quickly than *Allegro*.

Amoroso, see *Con amore*.

Andante, rather slowly and gently.

Andantino, not as slowly as *Andante*.

Animato, Con anima, with animation.

A piacere, see *Ad libitum*.

A poco a poco, Poco a poco, little by little, gradually.

Appassionata, Con passione, impassioned.

Assai, very (e.g., *Allegro assai*, very lively).

A tempo, Tempo primo, return to the original speed or tempo.

Ben marcato, well marked or accented.

Brillante, brilliantly.

Cantabile, in a singing style.

Con amore, Amoroso, lovingly.

Con anima, see *Animato*.

Con brio, brightly or vigorously.

Con dolore, see *Dolente*.

Con energia, Energico, energetically.

Con espressione, Espressivo, with expression.

Con forza, with force.

Con grazia, see *Grazioso*.

Con moto, Con spirito, with spirit.

Con passione, see *Appassionata*.

Con spirito, see *Con moto*.

Con tenerezza, with tenderness.

Crescendo (Cresc.), gradually becoming louder.

Da Capo (D.C.), repeat from the beginning.

Deciso, with precision.

Decrescendo (Decresc.), see *Diminuendo*.

Delicato, delicately.

Diminuendo (Dim.), Decrescendo, becoming softer.

Dolce, sweetly.

Dolente, Doloroso, Con dolore, with grief.

Doloroso, see *Dolente*.

E, Ed, and.

Energico, see *Con energia*.

Espressivo, see *Con espressione*.

f, see *Forte*.

ff, see *Fortissimo*.

fff, see *Forte possibile*.

Fine, the end (e.g., *D.C. al fine*, repeat from the beginning to the point marked *fine*).

Forte (f), loud.

Forte-piano (fp), loud, then becoming immediately soft.

Forte possibile (fff), as loud as possible.

Fortissimo (ff), very loud.

fp, see *Forte-piano*.

Fuoco, fire (e.g., *Con fuoco*, with fire).

Giocoso, gaily.

Giusto, see *Tempo giusto*.

Grandioso, in a grand style.

Grave, very slowly and solemnly. (See also *Largo*.)

Grazioso, Con grazia, gracefully.

Lamentoso, mournfully.

Larghetto, not as slowly as *Largo*.

Largo, very slowly. (See also *Adagio* and *Grave*. There is considerable difference of opinion as to which of these three terms indicates the slowest time. Any one of them can, therefore, be used to indicate "as slow as possible.")

Legato, smoothly.

Leggieramente, see *Leggiero*.

Leggiero, Leggieramente, lightly.

Lento, slowly.

Ma, but.

Maestoso, majestically.

Marcato, marked or accented.

Marziale, see *Alla marcia*.

Meno, less.

Mezzo forte (mf), not as loud as *forte* (*f*); i.e., moderately loud.

Mezzo piano (mp), not as soft as *piano* (*p*); i.e., moderately soft.

mf, see *Mezzo forte*.

M.M., Maelzel's Metronome. (Maelzel was a friend of Beethoven's who invented the metronome, a mechanical instrument used for setting tempo. The expression "M.M. ♩ =60", for example, means that a quarter note will receive the time value of the beat heard when the metronome is set at 60.)

Moderato (Modº), at a moderate speed.

Molto, very much (e.g., *Allegro molto*, very fast).

Morendo, dying away in time and tone.

Mosso, motion (e.g., *Meno mosso*, less motion, or slower).

mp, see *Mezzo piano*.

Non, not.

p, see *Piano*.

Pastorale, in a pastoral or quiet manner.

Pesante, heavily.

Piacevole, pleasantly.

Piangevole, plaintively.

Pianissimo (pp), very softly.

Piano (p), softly.

Piano possibile (ppp), as softly as possible.

Piu, more (e.g., *Piu mosso*, more movement, or quicker).

Poco, a little (e.g., *Poco allegro*, rather fast).

pp, see *Pianissimo*.

ppp, see *Piano possibile*.

Poco a poco, see *A poco a poco*.

Presto, very fast.

Quasi, as or like (e.g., *Quasi andante*, rather slowly).

Rallentando (Rall.), see *Ritardando*.

Religioso, in a devotional manner.

Repetizione, a repeat.

Risoluto, boldly.

Ritardando (Ritard. or Rit.), Rallentando (Rall.), gradually slower.

Ritenuto (Rit.), suddenly slower.

Rubato, see *Tempo rubato*.

Scherzando, Scherzo, playfully.

Semplice, with simplicty.

Senza, without (e.g., *Senza repetizione*, without repeats).

Serioso, in a serious manner.

Sforzando (sf), strongly accented.

Soave, gently.

Sostenuto, sustaining the tone.

Stringendo, increasing the tempo (often suddenly).

Tempo commodo, at a convenient pace.

Tempo di minuetto, in minuet time.

Tempo di valse, in waltz time.

Tempo giusto, Giusto, in exact time.

Tempo primo, see *A tempo*.

Tempo rubato, in robbed time. (The note values may be altered at the performer's pleasure for purposes of expression, provided that the time value of the whole measure is not altered.)

Tenuto (Ten.), hold a note, a sort of pause.

Tranquillo, in a quiet manner.

Troppo, too much (e.g., *Allegro ma non troppo*, quickly but not too quickly).

Veloce, see *Vivo*.

Vivace, lively and very quickly.

Vivo, Veloce, with vivacity.

Volti subito (V.S.), turn the page quickly.

INDEX OF THEORY

Accents, 7, 10
Accidentals, 82

Bar lines, 6
Barred eighth note, 57
Bars, 6; double, 6, 14; incomplete opening, 40-47
Beat values, 30, 53-61, 62, 71
Breve, 53

C major, key of, 88; scale of, 88
C, middle, 4
Cadence, points of, 7
Clefs, 3-4
Common time, 15
Crotchet, 6

D major, scale of, 89
Diminuendo, 12
Di, 83
Do, 4, 5, 9, 15, 82, 83, 89, 90, 91, 96
Dominant, 89, 91, 100
Dot, 30; dotted half note, 30; dotted half rest, 30;
    dotted quarter note, 71-76
Duration, 1

Eighth note, see *Notes*
Eighth rest, see *Rests*
Enharmonic change, 95-96
Expression, 1

F, scale of, 95
Fa, 89, 95, 101
Fi, 91, 100
Flats, 5, 82, 95, 100
Four-eight time, 57, 62
Four-four time, 53, 60, 62, 71
Four-two time, 53

G, key of, 89

Half note, see *Notes*
Half rest, see *Rests*

Key signatures, 5, 88, 89, 90, 95
Keyboard, piano, 2, 82, 88
Keynote, 15

La, 89
Leading note, 89
Leger lines, 4

Ma, 83
Measures, 6
Mediant, 89
Mi, 15, 83, 89; melodies starting on, 15-17
Middle C, 4
Minim, 6
Modulation, 90-102

Naturals, 83, 100, 101
Neumes, 1
Notation, 1
Notes, 3; whole notes, 6, 7, 53; half notes, 6,
    7, 30, 53-56; quarter notes, 6, 7, 71-76;
    eighth notes, 56-59, 62-70; beat values of
    notes, 7, 53-59; solfa names of notes, 89;
    technical names of notes, 89

Octave, 3

Pause sign, 23
Phrase mark, 7, 25
Piano keyboard, 2, 82, 88
Pitch, 1, 6

Quarter note, see *Notes*
Quarter rest, see *Rests*

Ra, 83
Re, 83, 89
Repeat signs, 23, 61, 67
Rests, whole, half, and quarter, 21-24, 30;
    eighth rest, 57, 62-70, 77-81; full bar's rest, 37
Rhythm, 1
Ri, 83

Scales, major, 88-102
Semibreve, 6
Semitone, 82, 88, 89
Sequence, 50
Sharps, 5, 82, 95, 100, 101
Signs, accent, 10; diminuendo, 12; double
    bar, 14; natural, 83, 100, 101; pause, 23;
    phrase, 25; repeat, 23, 61, 67; slur, 25;
    tie, 27
Slur, 25
So, 18, 89; melodies starting on, 18-20
Solfa, 88, 89; names, 89
Staff, 3
Stave, 1-3
Subdominant, 89, 95, 96, 101

Submediant, 89
Supertonic, 89
Syncopation, 29

Ta, 101
Terms, musical, 7, 109
Three-eight time, 57, 62
Three-four time, 34-37, 53, 60, 62, 71
Three-two time, 53
Ti, 89, 90, 100
Tie, 27-30
Time, common, 15

Time signatures, 6, 34, 53, 57, 60, 62, 71
Time values, 6, 27
Tonality, 90
Tone, 82, 88, 89
Tonic, 89
Tonic solfa, 4-5, 89, 91
Two-eight time, 57, 62
Two-four time, 37-39, 53, 62, 71
Two-two time, 53

Whole note, see *Notes*
Whole rest, see *Rests*

INDEX OF FORMS

Art songs, 77, 97, 100 108

Ballads, 42, 65, 66, 97, 99, 104

Carols, 20, 23, 26, 28, 39, 58, 62, 63, 68
Chants, 19, 29, 32, 38, 44
Chorales, 11, 23, 40, 47, 60, 67. See also *Hymns*
Concertos, 50, 66, 87, 104, 106

Dances, 16, 22, 23, 37, 52, 58, 66, 69, 70, 85, 91, 92

Fantasy, 102
Folk music, American, 35, 43; Austrian, 58; Bavarian, 23; Bohemian, 76; Cornish, 105; Croatian, 39; Czech, 32, 37, 92; Danish, 91; Dutch, 69, 73, 75; English, 11, 13, 14, 28, 41, 42, 49, 55, 56, 60, 63, 66, 68, 72, 79, 98, 105, 107; French, 13, 20, 22, 36, 38, 58; French Canadian, 34, 61, 62, 78; German, 47, 52, 64, 70, 80; Hungarian, 28; Irish, 65, 92; Latin American, 108; Lithuanian, 22; Magyar, 24; Polish, 18, 23, 25; Rhenish, 70; Russian, 16, 25, 27, 31, 46, 66, 69, 98; Serbian, 33; Spanish, 18; Swiss, 45; Thuringian, 49; Welsh, 10, 12, 50, 55; Yugo-Slavian, 100

Gavottes, 70, 85

Hymns, 10, 12, 14, 16, 17, 18, 26, 29, 32, 35, 36, 38, 48, 50, 54, 55, 56, 63, 68, 72, 75, 84, 93, 101, 103, 106. See also *Chorales*

Madrigal, 94
Marches, 74, 98
Minuets, 37, 58, 66
Musette, 85

Nocturnes, 19, 75

Operas, 14, 24, 33, 34, 45, 56, 64, 75, 76, 85, 86, 87, 93, 96, 99, 102
Oratorio, 67
Overtures, 10, 24, 56, 76, 86, 87

Quartets, 29, 70, 73, 85
Quintet, 51

Rhapsody, 67
Rounds, 49, 55, 56, 60

Sea shanties, 42, 43, 72
Sextets, 65, 87
Sonatas, 16, 99, 104
Suites, 29, 51, 80
Symphonies, 43, 61, 73, 76, 81, 84, 101, 106

Trios, 41, 51, 108

Valses, see *Waltzes*

Waltzes, 39, 52

INDEX OF COMPOSERS

BACH, J. S.
Arioso, Theme adapted from, 29
Christmas Oratorio, Chorale from, 67
Chorales, 47, 60
Morning Star, The (Chorale), 40
O Saviour Sweet, 103

BEETHOVEN
Eighth Symphony, Theme from, 84
Fifth Symphony, Theme from, 61
First Symphony, Theme from, 81
Hymn to Joy (Ninth Symphony), 106
Leonore Overture No. 3, Theme from, 56
Melodies, 44, 59
Morning Praise, 50
Night Song, 84
Quartet in A, Theme adapted from, 29
Sonata in C Major, Theme from, 16
Sonata in F Major, Theme from, 104
Sonata in G Major, Theme from, 99
Violin Concerto in D, Theme from, 104

BRAHMS
Academic Festival Overture, Theme from, 10
My Little Queen, 108
Piano Trio in B, Theme from, 41
Requiem, Theme from, 43
String Quartet in F, Theme from, 73
String Sextet in B^b, Theme from, 87

CHABRIER
Espana, Theme from, 67

CHOPIN
Fantasia Impromptu, Theme from, 102
Nocturne in G Minor, Theme from, 19
Valse in A^b, Theme from, 39

CORELLI
Tenth Concerto, Minuet from, 66

CORNELIUS
Monotone, The, 77

CRÜGER
From Thee All Skill and Science Flow, 55

FILITZ
Lead Us, Heavenly Father, 101
Winter Night, 15

GIBBONS, ORLANDO
Hymn, 48

GLUCK
Armide, Musette adapted from, 85

HANDEL
Fill Thou My Life, 56

HAUPTMANN
Christmas Song, 28
Roses I Bring, 31

HAVERGAL
Twenty-Third Psalm, 63

HAYDN
Farewell Symphony, Theme from, 101
String Quartet in B^b, Theme from, 85
String Quartet in E^b, Theme from, 70

KINKEL
Soldier's Farewell, The, 97

MARIE ANTOINETTE
Marie Antoinette's Song, 94

MASON, LOWELL
Lord, We Are Few, 29

MENDELSSOHN
Midsummer Night's Dream, Nocturne from, 75
Midsummer Night's Dream, Theme from Overture to, 86
Parting, 100
Ruy Blas, Theme from, 87

MONK, HENRY
Evening, 17

MOREY
Passing By, 97

MORLEY
Now is the Month of Maying, 94

MOUSSORGSKY
Pictures at an Exhibition, Theme from, 51

MOZART
Ave Verum, Excerpt from, 93
Clarinet Quintet, Theme adapted from, 51
Don Giovanni, Theme adapted from, 14
Eine Kleine Nachtmusik, Theme from, 80
Haffner Symphony, Theme adapted from, 76
Horn Sextet in F, Theme from, 65
Marriage of Figaro, Theme adapted from, 76
Melody, 85
Piano Concerto, Theme from, 50
Piano Trio in G, Theme adapted from, 108
Trio in E^b, Theme adapted from, 51

NEANDER, JOACHIM
Reverence, 16

NICOLAI
Wake, Awake—Chorale (adapted), 23

NICOLAI-BACH
Morning Star, The (Chorale), 40

PALESTRINA
Hosanna! 19
Strife is O'er, The, 36

PEACE
Submission, 12

PLEYEL
Minuet, 58
Sovereign Ruler of the Skies, 72
Themes, 17, 24

PURCELL
Faery Queen, Theme from, 45

SCHUBERT
Impromptu, 83
Impromptu, Theme from, 74
Symphony in C Major, Theme from, 73

SCHUMANN
Melody, 86
Piano Concerto in A Minor, Theme from, 87
Theme, 41

SPICKER
Linden in the Dale, The, 47

STRAUSS, JOHANN
Waltz Theme, 52

SULLIVAN
Admiral's Song, 64
Buttercup's Song, 96
He is an Englishman! 93
Let Us With a Gladsome Mind, 54

TSCHAIKOWSKY
Alleluia, 44
Pathétique Symphony, Theme from, 43
Piano Concerto in B^b Minor, Theme from, 106
Pique Dame, Excerpt from, 102
Romeo and Juliet, Theme from Overture to, 24

VERDI
La Traviata, Theme from, 33

WAGNER
Lohengrin, Excerpt from, 86

INDEX OF TITLES

TITLE	COMPOSER OR SOURCE	PAGE
ACADEMIC FESTIVAL OVERTURE, THEME FROM THE	BRAHMS	10
ADMIRAL'S SONG	SULLIVAN	64
ALLELUIA	TSCHAIKOWSKY	44
ALL YE THAT ARE GOOD FELLOWS	OLD ENGLISH BALLAD	42
ARIOSO, THEME ADAPTED FROM THE	J. S. BACH	29
ARMIDE, MUSETTE ADAPTED FROM	GLUCK	85
AURA LEE	OLD AMERICAN SONG	19
AVE VERUM, EXCERPT FROM THE	MOZART	93
BAILIFF'S DAUGHTER, THE	OLD ENGLISH BALLAD	104
BEE, THE	OLD ENGLISH ROUND	55
BLESSED STRANGER	POLISH CAROL	23
BLUE WAVES ARE TOSSING	BOHEMIAN FOLK SONG	76
BOUND TO ALABAMA	SEA SHANTY	43
BROKEN TRYST, THE	WELSH MELODY	12
BUTTERCUP'S SONG	SULLIVAN	96
CAPTIVE, THE	RUSSIAN FOLK SONG	31
CAROL	FRENCH	20
CHORALE	THOMMEN'S CHORALE BOOK	11
CHORALE	J. S. BACH	47
CHORALE	J. S. BACH	60
CHRISTMAS ORATORIO, CHORALE FROM THE	J. S. BACH	67
CHRISTMAS SONG	HAUPTMANN	28
CLARINET QUINTET, THEME ADAPTED FROM THE	MOZART	51
COSSACK DANCE		16
COUNTRY DANCE	BAVARIAN FOLK TUNE	23
CROATIAN CAROL	14TH CENTURY	39
CZECH FOLK DANCE		92
DANCERS, THE	SERBIAN FOLK SONG	33
DANISH FOLK DANCE		91
DANS TOUS LES CANTONS	FRENCH CANADIAN FOLK SONG	78
DEAR LITTLE SHAMROCK, THE	IRISH FOLK SONG	92
DON GIOVANNI, THEME ADAPTED FROM	MOZART	14
D'OÙ VIENS-TU, BERGÈRE?	FRENCH CANADIAN FOLK CAROL	62
DOWN IN THE VALLEY	KENTUCKY MOUNTAIN FOLK SONG	35
DUTCH DANCE TUNE		69
EAGLE, THE	ANONYMOUS	13
EIGHTH SYMPHONY, THEME FROM THE	BEETHOVEN	84
EINE KLEINE NACHTMUSIK, THEME FROM	MOZART	80
ESPANA, THEME FROM	CHABRIER	67
EVENING	HENRY MONK	17
EVENING SONG	WELSH MELODY	10
FAERY QUEEN, THEME FROM THE	PURCELL	45
FAITHFUL SAILOR	THE COBBLER'S OPERA	99

Title	Composer or Source	Page
Fantasia Impromptu, Theme from the	Chopin	102
Farewell Symphony, Theme from the	Haydn	101
Fifth Symphony, Theme from the	Beethoven	61
Fill Thou My Life	Haydn	56
First Symphony, Theme from the	Beethoven	81
Forty-Second Psalm, The	French Chant	32
From Thee All Skill and Science Flow	Crüger	55
Gai lon la, gai le rosier	French Canadian Folk Song	61
God Rest You Merry, Gentlemen	Old English Carol	68
Good-Night to You All	Old Round	49
Haffner Symphony, Theme adapted from the	Mozart	76
Hallelujah!	Spanish	26
He is an Englishman!	Sullivan	93
Hola!	German Folk Tune	80
Horn Sextet in F, Theme from the	Mozart	65
Hosanna!	Palestrina	19
How Can I Leave Thee?	Thuringian Folk Song	49
Hunting Song		11
Hymn	Orlando Gibbons	48
Hymn to Joy	Beethoven	106
I Love a Maiden Fair	Latin American Folk Song	108
Impromptu	Schubert	83
Impromptu, Theme from the	Schubert	74
Io Vivat	Dutch Folk Tune	73
King Arthur Had Three Sons	English Folk Song	79
La Traviata, Theme from	Verdi	33
Lead Us, Heavenly Father	Filitz	101
Leonore Overture No. 3, Theme from the	Beethoven	56
Let Us With a Gladsome Mind	Sullivan	54
Linden in the Dale, The	Spicker	47
Lithuanian Folk Dance		22
Little Man, The	Russian Folk Song	69
Lohengrin, Excerpt from	Wagner	86
London Watchman, The	Old English	105
Lonely Swan, The	Russian Folk Song	27
Lord, Thy Word Abideth	Bohemian Hymn	10
Lord, We Are Few	Lowell Mason	29
Manger, The	Austrian Carol	58
March of King James II	The Dancing Master	74
Marching Song	Russian Folk Song	98
Marie Antoinette's Song	Marie Antoinette	94
Marriage of Figaro, Theme adapted from the	Mozart	76
Massacre of the Macpherson, The		78
Melody	Beethoven	44
Melody	Beethoven	59
Melody	Mozart	85
Melody	Schumann	86

116

Title	Composer or Source	Page
Midsummer Night's Dream, Nocturne from	Mendelssohn	75
Midsummer Night's Dream, Theme from Overture to	Mendelssohn	86
Minuet	Old English	37
Minuet	Pleyel	58
Monotone, The	Cornelius	77
Morning Praise	Beethoven	50
Morning Star, The (Chorale)	Nicolai-Bach	40
My Little Queen	Brahms	108
Night	Czechoslovakian Folk Song	32
Night Song	Beethoven	84
Nocturne in G Minor, Theme from the	Chopin	19
Now is the Month of Maying	Morley	94
Now the Day is Over	Anonymous	14, 15
O Saviour Sweet	J. S. Bach	103
O Tempora! O Mores!	Old College Song	81
Oh, How Lovely is the Evening!	Old English Round	60
Oh No, John	Somerset Folk Song	107
Old English Carol		63
Old French Gavotte	Time of Louis XIV	70
Old Welsh Tune		55
On the Bridge of Avignon	French Folk Song	22
One Morning in the Spring	Old English	98
Parting	Mendelssohn	100
Passing By	Morey	97
Pathétique Symphony, Theme from the	Tschaikowsky	43
Piano Concerto, Theme from the	Mozart	50
Piano Concerto in A Minor, Theme from the	Schumann	87
Piano Concerto in B♭ Minor, Theme from the	Tschaikowsky	106
Piano Trio in B, Theme from the	Brahms	41
Piano Trio in G, Theme adapted from the	Mozart	108
Pictures at an Exhibition, Theme from	Moussorgsky	51
Pique Dame, Excerpt from	Tschaikowsky	102
Polish Hymn		18
Praise to the Lord	Stralsund Gesängbuch	35
Puer Nobis	Old Carol	26
Quartet in A, Theme adapted from the	Beethoven	29
Recollections	Czech Folk Song	37
Requiem, Theme from the	Brahms	43
Reverence	Joachim Neander	16
Rhenish Dance Tune		70
Robin Hood	Old English Ballad	66
Romeo and Juliet, Theme from the Overture to	Tschaikowsky	24
Roses I Bring	Hauptmann	31
Russian Dance		66
Ruy Blas, Theme from	Mendelssohn	87
Sea Shanty		42
Serenade	Russian Folk Song	46
Sherwood Forest	Old English	41

117

TITLE	COMPOSER OR SOURCE	PAGE
Sir John Franklin	Sea Shanty	72
Soldier's Farewell, The	Kinkel	97
Sonata in C Major, Theme from the	Beethoven	16
Sonata in F Major, Theme from the	Beethoven	104
Sonata in G Major, Theme from the	Beethoven	99
Song of the Emigrés	Old French	38
Song of the Exile	Irish Folk Song	65
Song of the Western Men	Cornish Song	105
Sovereign Ruler of the Skies	Pleyel	72
Spanish Folk Song		18
Spinning Song	German Folk Song	64
Stand for the King	Old French Tune	36
Strife is O'er, The	Palestrina	36
String Quartet in B♭, Theme adapted from	Haydn	85
String Quartet in E♭, Theme from the	Haydn	70
String Quartet in F, Theme from the	Brahms	73
String Sextet in B♭, Theme from the	Brahms	87
Submission	Peace	12
Symphony in C Major, Theme from the	Schubert	73
Tally Ho!	French Folk Tune	13
Tenth Concerto, Minuet from the	Corelli	66
Thanksgiving Hymn	Old Netherlands Folk Song	75
Theme	Pleyel	17
Theme	Pleyel	24
Theme	Schumann	41
Thou Fillest My Heart	German	52
Trio in E♭, Theme adapted from the	Mozart	51
Twenty-Third Psalm, The	Havergal	63
Un Canadien errant	French Canadian Folk Song	34
Un Flambeau	Old French Carol	58
Valse in A♭, Theme from the	Chopin	39
Veni Sancte Spiritus	13th Century Chant	38
Violin Concerto in D, Theme from the	Beethoven	104
Volga, The	Russian Folk Song	25
Wake, Awake—Chorale (adapted)	Nicolai	23
Waltz Theme	Johann Strauss	52
Wanderer, The	Hungarian Folk Song	28
Watchers, The	Polish Folk Song	25
Welsh Hymn		50
When the Wind is in the East	Old English Folk Tune	28
White Sand	Old English Round	56
Windmill, The	English (16th Century)	14
Winter Night	Filitz	15
Winter Song	Magyar Folk Tune	24
Wishing Well, The	Yugo-Slavian Folk Song	100
Wreath, The	Old English Song	107
Ye Watchers and Ye Holy Ones	17th Century Melody	68
Yodelling Song	Swiss Folk Tune	45
Young Heir, The	Old English	65